CROSS-DEVICE WEB SEARCH

Cross-device Web Search is the first book to examine cross-device search behavior, which takes place when people utilize multiple devices and several sessions to research the same topic.

Providing a comprehensive examination of cross-device search behaviors, the book also models and analyses their most important features and, by doing so, helps to elucidate the motivations behind such behaviors. Drawing on a variety of methods and sources, including system design, user experiments, and qualitative and quantitative analysis, the book introduces cross-device search, relates it to relevant conceptual models, and identifies cross-device search topics. Providing discussion of a comprehensive range of behaviors in the context of cross-device search, including querying, gazing, clicking, and touching, the book also presents the design and development of a system to support cross-device search, explores cross-device search behavior modeling, and predicts users' search performance.

Cross-device Web Search will be of great interest to academics and students situated in the fields of library and information science, computer science, and management science. The book should also provide fascinating insights to practitioners and others interested in information search retrieval, information seeking behavior, and human–computer interaction communities.

Dan Wu (Ph.D) is a Professor at Wuhan University, China. Her research interests include information retrieval, information behavior, and human–computer interaction. One of her most important publications is *Mobile Search Behaviors: An In-depth Analysis based on Contexts, APPs and Devices*, published by Morgan & Claypool.

Jing Dong (Ph.D) is an assistant professor at the School of Information Management, Central China Normal University. She obtained her Ph.D degree in Information Science at Wuhan University. She was a visiting scholar at the

University of Pittsburgh. She is interested in research areas of information-seeking behavior and human–computer interaction. She has published over 20 papers in peer-reviewed journals, such as *Information Processing & Management* and *Journal of the Association for Information Science and Technology*, and conference proceedings such as SIGIR and iConference.

Shaobo Liang is an assistant professor at the School of Information Management at Wuhan University. His research interests lie in understanding user information-seeking behavior, mobile search behavior, and cross-device search. He has published over 20 papers in academic journals and conferences.

CROSS-DEVICE WEB SEARCH

Dan Wu, Jing Dong, and Shaobo Liang

LONDON AND NEW YORK

First published 2022
by Routledge
605 Third Avenue, New York, NY 10158

and by Routledge
2 Park Square, Milton Park, Abingdon, Oxon, OX14 4RN

Routledge is an imprint of the Taylor & Francis Group, an informa business

© 2022 Dan Wu, Jing Dong and Shaobo Liang

The right of Dan Wu, Jing Dong and Shaobo Liang to be identified as author of this work has been asserted in accordance with sections 77 and 78 of the Copyright, Designs and Patents Act 1988.

All rights reserved. No part of this book may be reprinted or reproduced or utilised in any form or by any electronic, mechanical, or other means, now known or hereafter invented, including photocopying and recording, or in any information storage or retrieval system, without permission in writing from the publishers.

Trademark notice: Product or corporate names may be trademarks or registered trademarks, and are used only for identification and explanation without intent to infringe.

Library of Congress Cataloging-in-Publication Data
A catalog record for this title has been requested

ISBN: 978-0-367-19311-9 (hbk)
ISBN: 978-0-367-19313-3 (pbk)
ISBN: 978-0-429-20167-7 (ebk)

DOI: 10.4324/9780429201677

Typeset in Bembo
by SPi Technologies India Pvt Ltd (Straive)

Access the Support Material: www.routledge.com/9780367193133

CONTENTS

List of Figures	*ix*
List of Tables	*xi*
Support Material	*xiii*

1	**Introduction to Cross-device Search**	1
	1.1 Background	1
	1.2 Key Terms	2
	1.2.1 Cross-device/Cross-screen	3
	1.2.2 Multi-session Search	3
	1.2.3 Cross-session Search	3
	1.2.4 Cross-device Search	4
	1.2.5 Successive Search	4
	1.2.6 Exploratory Search	5
	1.3 Cross-device Search Study Methods	5
	1.4 Plan of the Book	6
2	**Theories Relating to Cross-device Search**	10
	2.1 Exploratory Search Theory	10
	2.1.1 Definition of Exploratory Search	10
	2.1.2 Models of Exploratory Search	11
	2.2 Successive Search Theory	12
	2.2.1 Spink's Theory of Successive Search	12
	2.2.2 Extension Theory of Successive Search	13
	2.3 Theoretical Models Supporting Cross-device Search Research	14
	2.3.1 Cross-device Taxonomy	14

vi Contents

	2.3.2	INFEX Framework	15
	2.3.3	Cross-device Search Pattern Model	16
2.4	Summary		17

3	Cross-device Search Topics		20
3.1	Existing Exploration on Cross-device Search Topics		20
	3.1.1	Subjects in Cross-device Search	21
	3.1.2	Task Type	21
	3.1.3	Task Complexity Measurement	23
3.2	Crowdsourcing Survey on Cross-device Search Topics		24
	3.2.1	Motivation	24
	3.2.2	Crowdsourcing Platforms	24
	3.2.3	Survey Design	25
	3.2.4	Respondent Backgrounds	29
3.3	Cross-Device Search Topic Identification		29
	3.3.1	Coding Topic Features	29
	3.3.2	Subject, Task Type and Complexity of Topics	32
	3.3.3	Context of Topics	34
	3.3.4	Intent and Motivation of Topics	36
	3.3.5	Process of Topic Search	39
3.4	Cross-device Search Topic Collection Development		41
	3.4.1	Correlation among Topic and Context Features	41
	3.4.2	Developing Topic Collection based on Correlations	43
3.5	Summary		47

4	Cross-device Search Support Techniques and Systems		51
4.1	Introduction of Existing Cross-device Search Systems		51
	4.1.1	Cross-device Support System in Industry	51
	4.1.2	Cross-device Support Systems in Academic	52
4.2	Cross-device Search Support Techniques		53
	4.2.1	Cross-device Tracking Techniques	53
	4.2.2	Cross-device Search Support Methods Based on Context	54
	4.2.3	Cross-device Search-Related Patents	55
4.3	Cross-device Search-Related Algorithms		56
4.4	Cross-device Search Systems Introduction and Development		56
4.5	Summary		58

5	Cross-device Search Behaviors		61
5.1	Related Work on Cross-device Search Behaviors		61
	5.1.1	Multi-session and Cross-session Search Behaviors	61
	5.1.2	Interaction and Search Behaviors in Cross-device Scenarios	63

Contents **vii**

5.2	Cross-device Search Experiment Design	64
	5.2.1 Research Motivation	64
	5.2.2 Theoretical Background	66
	5.2.3 Simulating Cross-device Search Motivations	68
	5.2.4 Experiment Procedure	70
	5.2.5 Participant Demographics	73
	5.2.6 Data Collection	74
	5.2.7 Data Analysis	77
5.3	Querying in Cross-device Search	78
	5.3.1 Basic Query Characteristics in Cross-device Search	78
	5.3.2 Query Reformulation in Cross-device Search	81
	5.3.3 Query Semantics Characteristics in Cross-device Search	85
5.4	Clicking in Cross-device Search	87
	5.4.1 Click Behavior Measurement	87
	5.4.2 Click Characteristics during the Cross-device Search	88
5.5	Cursor Movements and Touching in Cross-device Search	89
	5.5.1 Desktop Cursor Movements in Cross-device Search	89
	5.5.2 Mobile Touch Interactions (MTI) in Cross-device Search	94
5.6	Gazing in Cross-device Search	96
	5.6.1 Eye Tracking Analysis of Search Behavior	96
	5.6.2 Characteristics of Eye Movement in Cross-device Search	98
5.7	Effect Size on Observable Cross-device Search Behavior	99
5.8	Cognition of Cross-device Search	102
	5.8.1 Subjective Evaluation of Cross-device Search	102
	5.8.2 Search Strategies of Cross-device Search	103
5.9	Summary	105
6	Cross-device Search Behavior Modeling	113
6.1	Review of Cross-device Search-Related Behavior Modeling	113
	6.1.1 The approach of Search Behavior Modeling	113
	6.1.2 Cross-session Search Behavior Modeling	114
	6.1.3 Cross-device Search Behavior Modeling	114
6.2	Modeling Cross-device Search Behavior under Different Motivations	115
	6.2.1 Features	115
	6.2.2 Dataset	116
	6.2.3 Classifier	116
	6.2.4 Training	117

viii Contents

	6.3	Analysis of Model Performance Change	119
		6.3.1 Cross-device Search Behavior Model of Controlled Motivation	119
		6.3.2 Cross-device Search Behavior Model of Autonomous Motivation	119
	6.4	Analysis of Feature Importance	120
		6.4.1 Important Features of the Superior Model of Controlled Motivation	120
		6.4.2 Important Features of Superior Model of Autonomous Motivation	121
	6.5	Summary	122
7		Discussion and Conclusion	126
	7.1	Characteristics of Cross-device Search Topics Revealing Information Needs	126
	7.2	Effect of Motivation on Cross-device Search Behaviors	128
	7.3	Effective Method of Modeling Cross-device Search under Different Motivations	130
	7.4	Implications of Cross-device Search under Different Motivations	131
	7.5	Insight on Cross-device Search Studies	132
	7.6	Conclusion	132
	7.7	Summary	135
Index			*137*

FIGURES

1.1	Example of a cross-device search	4
3.1	Search subjects of cross-device search topics	33
3.2	Device switch demand for cross-device search topics	38
3.3	Switching intervals of cross-device search topics	41
3.4	Topic structure and example	44
4.1	Interface of AirDrop on Mac	52
4.2	The login page and search result page of CAFE	58
4.3	The design idea of CAFE	58
4.4	The search results re-ranking of CAFE	59
5.1	Experiment procedure	72
5.2	Basic query characteristics of pre-switch and post-switch searches	79
5.3	Basic query characteristics over the whole search	80
5.4	Query reformulation occurrence of pre-switch and post-switch searches	83
5.5	Query reformulation occurrence over the whole search	84
5.6	QVR of pre-switch and post-switch searches	86
5.7	Query semantics over the whole search	86
5.8	Click characteristics of pre-switch and post-switch searches	88
5.9	Click characteristics over the whole search	90
5.10	Cursor movement frequency of pre-switch and post-switch searches	92
5.11	Cursor movement speed of pre-switch and post-switch searches	92
5.12	Cursor movements over the whole search	94
5.13	MTI frequency of pre-switch and post-switch searches	95
5.14	MTI speed of pre-switch and post-switch searches	95
5.15	MTI over the whole search	97
5.16	Eye movements of pre-switch and post-switch searches	99
5.17	Eye movements over the whole search	100

x Figures

5.18	Comparison of subjective evaluation between pre-search and post-search	102
6.1	F1 scores of search behavior models of controlled motivation	120
6.2	F1 scores of search behavior model of autonomous motivation	120
6.3	Feature importance of baseline and superior models of controlled motivation	121
6.4	Feature importance of baseline and superior models of autonomous motivation	122

TABLES

1.1	Research methods in previous research about cross-device search	5
3.1	Faceted classification of tasks (Li & Belkin, 2008) (WT refers to Work Task, ST refers to Search Task)	22
3.2	Revised framework of Bloom's Taxonomy (Krathwohl, 2002)	24
3.3	Cross-device search experience survey	25
3.4	Demographics of participants	30
3.5	Coding scheme	31
3.6	Task types of cross-device search topics	34
3.7	Task complexity of cross-device search topics	35
3.8	Device switch of cross-device search topics	36
3.9	Queries issued in cross-device search topics	39
3.10	Visited page of cross-device search topics	40
3.11	Contingency coefficients among features of topic	41
3.12	Contingency coefficient among features of topic context	42
3.13	Contingency coefficients between topic and context	43
3.14	<outcome> and <mental activities> corresponding to <cognitive>	45
3.15	Summary of eight switching reasons	47
4.1	Some patents of cross-device search	55
4.2	Cross-device related algorithm	57
5.1	Designed scenarios of cross-device search motivation	69
5.2	Content of the search task and instructions	71
5.3	Participant number of the motivation	73
5.4	Demographics of 59 participants	73
5.5	Data types and collecting methods	74
5.6	CAFE log examples of different events	75
5.7	Data types of different gaze events	75
5.8	Questions of pre- & post-surveys	76

xii Tables

5.9	Interview questions	76
5.10	Measures of basic query characteristics	78
5.11	Results of two-way ANOVA on query characteristics	81
5.12	Types of query reformulation	82
5.13	Results of two-way ANOVA on query reformulation	84
5.14	Measures of query semantics	85
5.15	Results of two-way ANOVA on query semantics	87
5.16	Measures of clicks	88
5.17	Results of two-way ANOVA on clicks	90
5.18	Measures of cursor movements	91
5.19	Results of two-way ANOVA on cursor movements	93
5.20	Measures of MTI	95
5.21	Results of two-way ANOVA on MTI	97
5.22	Measures of eye movements	98
5.23	Results of two-way ANOVA on eye movements	100
5.24	Effect size of controlled motivation on cross-device search behavior	101
5.25	Effect size of autonomous motivation on cross-device search behavior	101
5.26	Results of paired samples T-test on subjective evaluation	103
5.27	Summary of the effects of motivation on cross-device search behaviors	106
6.1	Features of modeling	115
6.2	Baseline model performance of three classifiers	118
6.3	Models and corresponding features	119
6.4	Summary of important feature groups and features of cross-device search behavior models under controlled and autonomous motivations	123

SUPPORT MATERIAL

The Support Material online is the Cross-device Search Topic Collection. In Chapter 3, the analysis of the crowdsourcing survey on real-situation cross-device searches extracts the features of cross-device search topics, and the method of designing cross-device search topics/tasks is proposed. The structure of topic is described in the form of XML with primary tags of <number>, <subject>, <type>, <complexity>, <narrative>, <search system>, <goal>, <device switch> and <switching reasons>, covering the features of topic itself and topic context. The topic collection consists of 343 topics extracted from the survey and additional topics extended from real searches. Researchers are welcome to utilize the topic collection in their user studies and be inspired for designing search tasks.

Visit the Support Material: www.routledge.com/9780367193119

1

INTRODUCTION TO CROSS-DEVICE SEARCH

1.1 Background

With the development of smart devices, people have embraced not only mobile phones, desktops, laptops, and tablets, but also smart TVs, wearable watches, and other devices. Cross-device ownership refers to the fact that individuals own and use multiple digital devices from which they can access content, play games, watch TV, and carry out other activities (Connie, 2017). According to market data, 77% of online users own at least one mobile and one PC device, and 44% of online users own at least one smartphone, one tablet, and one PC device (Verto, 2017). Users' human–computer interaction tasks will occur on different devices and has become a common phenomenon.

With increasing device functions and types, users' network search methods are increasingly diversified. Under the environment of cross-device ownership, users' search activities will span different types of devices and may switch among various devices. Users' complex search tasks also may span a long time, often needing multiple search sessions, and occurring on different devices (Han, Zhen, & He, 2015). For instance, a person used his/her smartphone to search for information about a stock in the morning. Then, he/she came to the office and used the desktop to search for relevant financial news and to buy stocks. After dinner, he/she sits on the sofa at home and uses an iPad to search for stock price trends. This is a typical example of a cross-device search.

In the above example, the user's search activity occurs on different devices, and a search task also occurs in multiple search sessions. Nowadays, many, the various options in search devices provide a diverse ecosystem of personal devices for cross-device search (Geronimo, Husmann, & Norrie, 2016). The analysis of logs from the United States local market showed that about 5% of users possess more than one device and that queries issued by multi-device

DOI: 10.4324/9780429201677-1

users account for over 16% (Montañez, White, & Huang, 2014). Search across multiple devices by an individual has become a common usage pattern since people can query search providers almost any time and from anywhere (Wang, Huang, & White, 2013).

According to CNNIC data (2020), 99.7% of Chinese netizens use mobile phones to surf the Internet. The proportion of using desktop, laptops, TVs, and tablets to access the Internet is 32.8%, 28.2%, 24.0%, and 22.9%, respectively. Interacting with two or more devices is the norm for multi-device users, and using a mobile phone first does not mean the mobile phone is the only device used. The majority of multi-device users show a preference for using different devices for searching.

In previous studies (MacKay & Watters, 2008a; MacKay & Watters, 2008b; Morris, Ringel Morris, & Venolia, 2008; Sellen, Murphy, & Shaw, 2002), researchers investigated the cross-device search behavior of specific groups (such as knowledge workers, students, researchers, etc.), through a combination of interviews, log data, and other research methods. These studies show that cross-device searches will be triggered by various search topics and tasks, and searchers will use different methods to save information (such as bookmarks, notes, e-mail to themselves, etc.) before resuming the previous search process and continuing the search. However, these methods cannot help users search on different devices better. Karlson, Meyers, Jacobs, Johns, & Kane, (2009) also point out that tasks cannot be easily carried over between devices due to lack of support.

As stated, with the ubiquitous popularity of mobile devices, cross-device search is a current phenomenon all over the world; thus, the topics and the outcomes of this book are relevant not just to China but to the whole world. This book can fulfill various needs. To academics, this book will stimulate research interests regarding information retrieval, information-seeking behavior, and HCI communities. The findings about cross-device search behavior and the models we will develop can enrich existing research in the search domain. To internet industries, this book can provide implications on improving search surface and function design. To the general public who wants to know about cross-device search behavior, this book can provide a systematic and comprehensive introduction, including theoretical, technical, and empirical studies.

The topic of this book is innovative. Currently, there is no book concerning cross-device search behavior existing on the market. Therefore, this book is equipped with a unique competitive strength in that it should be the first about cross-device search behavior research.

1.2 Key Terms

In this part, we introduce several important key terms, which are closely related to the research topic. The key terms we list here will appear in this book. At the beginning of this book, we hope to introduce the key words to the readers and help them understand these concepts.

1.2.1 Cross-device/Cross-screen

As mentioned above, as users have more smart devices, they often interact on different devices over a period of time, and there is a certain correlation between these interactions on different devices. Of course, it can also be said that the users' interactions are on different screens.

Neate, Jones, & Evans (2017) studied user interactions on smartphones and smart TVs, and defined multi-device systems as those which involve computing experiences that span two or more devices. Another related key term is cross-screen. In Google's report (2012), they defined "cross-screen" as the usage of a second screen (or more than one screen) for related work sequentially or for related work simultaneously.

In this book, "cross-screen" means having or utilizing more than one screen at the same time. From the above, the concepts of cross-device and cross-screen are very similar.

1.2.2 Multi-session Search

Previous studies (Pavani & Teja, 2015) have defined the search session as "the series of both clicked and unclicked URLs from user click-through logs." Jansen, Spink, & Kathuria (2006) classify the search session "from a contextual viewpoint as a series of interactions by the user toward addressing a single information need." Church, Smyth, Cotter, & Bradley (2007) concluded that a search session is "a session where the user has engaged in at least some search activity."

In users' daily lives, some information needs will not be completed within a short time. According to the definition of a search session, users' search activities may be distributed across multiple search sessions. MacKay & Watters (2008a) defined multi-session searches as those that have a specific and defined goal and that require more than one web session to complete. Kotov, Bennett, White, Dumais, & Teevan (2011) also found that there are complex tasks requiring many queries spanning multiple search sessions.

1.2.3 Cross-session Search

The search session has also been defined as "a sequence of queries issued by a single user within a specific time limit" (Boldi et al., 2008). Similar to the concept of multi-session search, a cross-session task consists of a series of queries that corresponds to a distinct high-level information need (Kotov et al., 2011).

There are often a series of search activities to achieve a single goal, but spread across multiple sessions. This can be regarded as either a multi-session search or cross-session search. In our book, multi-session and cross-session searches can be regarded as a series of queries corresponding to a distinct high-level information need that is segmented into short time units.

1.2.4 Cross-device Search

Facing a complex search task, searchers may use different devices to find information at different times and locations (Wu & Liang, 2018).

Wang, Huang, & White (2013) studied users' cross-device search behavior using large-scale log data, and defined the cross-device search as a set of seven tuples, including search history, query before device transition, query after device transition, previous device, current device, search session before device transition and search session after device transition. Montañez et al. (2014) proposed a related concept, "device transition," which means that consecutive queries are issued on different devices. Figure 1.1 shows an example of a cross-device search. While a user was planning a trip to New York, he/she searched for "flight to New York" on a mobile phone, and searched for "Italian foods in New York." In the evening, he/she continued to search for "Mexican foods in New York."

In our previous study (Wu & Liang, 2018), the cross-device search was defined as users submitting queries on different devices over a period of time. A cross-device search consists of a pre-switch session and a post-switch session; in other words, at least two sessions are conducted on separate devices.

1.2.5 Successive Search

Spink (1996) initially pointed out the concept of "successive search," which refers to the process of generating repeated and continuous search segments for an evolving information problem over a period of time (Spink et al., 1998). Successive search consists of multiple continuous search segments. "Segment" is understood as an alternative concept of search session, and refers to a series of interactive behaviors between users and search systems, divided into segments in a time period. Successive search has the following characteristics: (1) In a successive search, although there are multiple search segments, all the searches generally point to the same information problem. (2) An important reason why users engage in successive search behavior is to optimize the previous search segment. (3) Users often regard the previous search segment in a successive search as an experiment and exploration. The search experience in the previous segment can help users determine more effective key words in subsequent searches. (4) Compared with the previous segment, users often produce more search activities in the following

FIGURE 1.1 Example of a cross-device search

Introduction to Cross-device Search **5**

segment, such as more key words and access to more search results. (5) With a successive search, the number of search results accessed by users does not necessarily decline, and the retrieval accuracy does not necessarily improve significantly, but users will have a clearer understanding of their information problems.

1.2.6 Exploratory Search

Exploratory search is regarded as a loosely defined concept with a definition that evolves with the development of systems (Palagi, Gandon, Giboin, & Troncy, 2017). Marchionini (2006) took the first step, of characterizing and conceptualizing exploratory search. White & Roth (2009) pointed out that exploratory search is not only the act of exploration, but also involves complex cognitive activities associated with knowledge acquisition and the development of intellectual skills. Exploratory searches include an abundance of behaviors beyond typical search behavior, such as exploration, uncertainty, creativity, knowledge discovery, and learning (Hendahewa & Shah, 2017).

1.3 Cross-device Search Study Methods

In the existing research, many scholars have investigated cross-device search in depth. We selected some important studies in particular and analyzed the research methods and participants/users scales in these studies, as shown in Table 1.1.

In general, research on cross-device search mainly includes quantitative research and qualitative research. Quantitative research primarily involves the use of user

TABLE 1.1 Research methods in previous research about cross-device search

Previous Studies	Research Method	Participants/Users	Participants Scale/ Dataset
Han, Zhen, & He (2015)	Controlled-user experiment	Students	24 participants
Wang, Huang, & White (2013)	Log-based study	General users of search engines	39,081 users
Chen & Li (2017)	User experiment	General users owning multiple devices	14 participants
Montañez et al. (2014)	Log-based study	General users in the USA	33,221,253 users
Karlson et al. (2009)	Log-based study Interview	Information workers	16 participants (4 for interview)
Wu et al. (2020)	User experiment Log-based study Survey	Students from Wuhan University	34 participants
Wu, Dong, & Liu (2019)	Crowdsourcing Survey	General users owning multiple devices	343 participants
Cecchinato, Sellen, Shokouhi, & Smyth (2016)	Diary study Interview	General users in the UK	16 participants

(Continued)

6 Introduction to Cross-device Search

TABLE 1.1 (Continued)

Previous Studies	Research Method	Participants/Users	Participants Scale/Dataset
Kane et al. (2009)	Survey Log-based study	smartphone users : employees at a technology company	175 participants for the survey and 14 participants for the log-based study
Zagermann et al. (2020)	User experiments Log-based study Survey	Students	24 participants

experiments, log data, and survey methods. Large-scale log data research helps us understand the cross-device search behavior of most users. For example, Montañez et al. (2014) and Wang, Huang, & White (2013) have investigated large-scale users.

User experiments are often combined with log studies. Researchers implement different experiments to record the behavior data of users in the experiments and study the characteristics of their cross-device search behavior.

Table 1.1 shows that the hybrid research method has gradually been used more often, and scholars have adopted both quantitative and qualitative research methods in their research. For example, Karlson et al. (2009) not only analyzed log data but also obtained a more in-depth understanding through interviews.

Large-scale log data collection is the most common method in the research of user information behavior, especially in the research of information-searching behavior. It can provide a large amount of anonymous user log data, but it cannot mine the deep reasons behind user behavior for the information reflected by log data. Questionnaire surveys are a common empirical research method. However, this method cannot collect the log data of users interacting with smartphones in a real environment, resulting in some defects in both authenticity and objectivity.

1.4 Plan of the Book

In this book, we will study users' cross-device behaviors. User experiments were conducted to collect users' log data, eye-tracking data, and other behavior data. Crowdsourcing, interviews, and questionnaires were also used to collect different data aspects.

In Chapter 2, we discuss theories and conceptual models related to the cross-device search, aiming to understand cross-device search behavior from a theoretical point of view.

In Chapter 3, we explore cross-device search behavior through the characteristics of cross-device search topics. This chapter collects descriptions of real-situation cross-device search experiences with a global crowdsourcing survey.

In Chapter 4, we introduce existing techniques and systems for cross-device search. We first give a brief review in the domain of cross-device search systems. Then, we introduce how to identify unique users in cross-device search settings. Lastly, we introduce the Cross-device Access and Fusion Engine, a self-developed cross-device search engine. This search engine was used in the experiment in our study.

In Chapter 5, we further explore cross-device search behavior under different motivations. Four motivations are classified as controlled and autonomous motivations, according to the classic psychological theory. This chapter conducts a controlled experiment and analyzes the effects of motivation on cross-device search behavior.

Chapter 6 performs the cross-device search behavior modeling under controlled and autonomous motivations using the cross-device search behavior features covered in Chapter 5. The chapter aims to analyze the important behavioral features that distinguish cross-device search under different motivations.

Chapter 7 discusses the results of the empirical study. According to the results of cross-device search topics, this chapter discusses the characteristics of cross-device search information need through the characteristics of cross-device search topics. Then, this chapter discusses the implication of this book's findings, as well as its limitations and the prospects for future work.

Reference

Boldi, P., Bonchi, F., Castillo, C., Donato, D., Gionis, A., & Vigna, S. (2008, October). The query-flow graph: Model and applications. In *Proceedings of the 17th ACM Conference on Information and Knowledge Management* (pp. 609–618).

Cecchinato, M. E., Sellen, A., Shokouhi, M., & Smyth, G. (2016, May). Finding email in a multi-account, multi-device world. In *Proceedings of the 2016 CHI Conference on Human Factors in Computing Systems* (pp. 1200–1210).

Chen, X. A., & Li, Y. (2017). Improv: An input framework for improvising cross-device interaction by demonstration. *ACM Transactions on Computer-Human Interaction (TOCHI), 24*(2), 1–21.

Church, K., Smyth, B., Cotter, P., & Bradley, K. (2007). Mobile information access: A study of emerging search behavior on the mobile internet. *ACM Transactions on the Web (TWEB), 1*(1), 1–38.

CNNIC. (2020). The 47th China statistical report on Internet development. Retrieved from: http://www.cac.gov.cn/2021-02/03/c_1613923423079314.htm.

Connie, H. (2017). The state of cross-device ownership. https://vertoanalytics.com/chart-week-state-cross-device-ownership/

Geronimo, L. D., Husmann, M., & Norrie, M. C. (2016). Surveying personal device ecosystems with cross-device applications in mind. In *Proceedings of the 5th ACM International Symposium on Pervasive Displays* (pp. 220–227). New York: ACM.

Google. (2012). The New Multi-Screen World Study. Retrieved November 25, 2014, from, https://www.thinkwithgoogle.com/research-studies/the-new-multi-screen-wo

Han, S., Zhen, Y., & He, D. (2015). Understanding and supporting cross-device web search for exploratory tasks with mobile touch interactions. *ACM Transactions on Information Systems, 33*(4), 1–34. doi:10.1145/2738036

Hendahewa, C., & Shah, C. (2017). Evaluating user search trails in exploratory search tasks. *Information Processing & Management, 53*(4), 905-–922. doi:10.1016/j.ipm.2017.04.001.

Jansen, B.J., Spink, A., & Kathuria,V. (2006). How to define searching sessions on web search engines. In *Proceedings of the 8th Knowledge Discovery on the Web International Conference on Advances in Web Mining and Web Usage Analysis* (pp. 92–109). New York: Springer-Verlag.

Kane, S. K., Karlson, A. K., Meyers, B. R., Johns, P., Jacobs, A., & Smith, G. (2009, August). Exploring cross-device web use on PCs and mobile devices. In *IFIP Conference on Human-Computer Interaction* (pp. 722–735). Berlin, Heidelberg: Springer.

Karlson, A. K., Meyers, B. R., Jacobs, A., Johns, P., & Kane, S. K. (2009, May). Working overtime: Patterns of smartphone and PC usage in the day of an information worker. In *International Conference on Pervasive Computing* (pp. 398–405). Berlin, Heidelberg: Springer.

Kotov, A., Bennett, P. N., White, R. W., Dumais, S. T., & Teevan, J. (2011, July). Modeling and analysis of cross-session search tasks. In *Proceedings of the 34th International ACM SIGIR Conference on Research and Development in Information Retrieval* (pp. 5–14).

MacKay, B., & Watters, C. (2008a). Exploring multi-session web tasks. In *Proceedings of the SIGCHI Conference on Human Factors in Computing Systems (CHI '08)* (pp. 1187–1196). New York: Association for Computing Machinery.

MacKay, B., & Watters, C. (2008b). Understanding and supporting multi-session web tasks. *Proceedings of the American Society for Information Science and Technology, 45*(1), 1–13.

Marchionini, G. (2006). Exploratory search: From finding to understanding. *Communication ACM, 49*(4), 41–46. doi:10.1145/1121949.1121979

Montañez, G. D., White, R. W., & Huang, X. (2014). Cross-device search. In *Proceedings of the 23rd ACM International Conference on Information and Knowledge Management* (pp. 1669–1678). New York: ACM.

Morris, D., Ringel Morris, M., & Venolia, G. (2008, April). SearchBar: A search-centric web history for task resumption and information re-finding. In *Proceedings of the SIGCHI Conference on Human Factors in Computing Systems* (pp. 1207–1216).

Neate, T., Jones, M., & Evans, M. (2017). Cross-device media: A review of second screening and multi-device television. *Personal and Ubiquitous Computing, 21*(2), 391–405.

Palagi, E., Gandon F., Giboin, A., & Troncy, R. (2017). A survey of definitions and models of exploratory search. In *Proceedings of the 2017 ACM Workshop on Exploratory Search and Interactive Data Analytics.* (pp. 3–8). doi:10.1145/3038462.3038465

Sellen, A. J., Murphy, R., & Shaw, K. L. (2002, April). How knowledge workers use the web. In *Proceedings of the SIGCHI Conference on Human Factors in Computing Systems* (pp. 227–234).

Spink, A. (1996). Multiple search sessions model of end-user behavior: An exploratory study. *Journal of the American Society for Information Science, 47*(8), 603–609.

Spink, A., Bateman, J., & Griesdorf, H. (1998). Successive searching behaviour during information retrieval (IR) interaction: Development of a new line of research. In *Proceedings of the 26th Annual Meeting of the Canadian Association for Information Science* (pp. 401–415).

Verto. (2017). Cross-device and mobile consumers: Who are they and where do they spend time?. https://insights.vertoanalytics.com/cross-device-and-mobile-consumers-webinar-deck.

Wang, Y., Huang, X., & White, R. W. (2013, February). Characterizing and supporting cross-device search tasks. In *Proceedings of the Sixth ACM International Conference on Web Search and Data Mining* (pp. 707–716).

White, R. W., & Roth, R. A. (2009). Exploratory search: Beyond the query-response paradigm. *Synthesis Lectures on Information Concepts, Retrieval, and Services, 1*(1), 1–98. doi:10.2200/S00174ED1V01Y200901ICR003

Wu, D., Dong, J., & Liu, C. (2019). Exploratory study of cross-device search tasks. *Information Processing & Management, 56*(6), 102073.

Wu, D., Dong, J., Tang, Y., & Capra, R. (2020). Understanding task preparation and resumption behaviors in cross-device search. *Journal of the Association for Information Science and Technology, 71*, 887–901. doi:10.1002/asi.24307

Pavani, M., & Teja, G. R. (2015). Online clustering algorithm for restructuring user web search results. In Satapathy, S., Biswal, B., Udgata, S., & Mandal, J. (Eds.) *Proceedings of the 3rd International Conference on Frontiers of Intelligent Computing: Theory and Applications (FICTA)* 2014. Cham: Springer.(pp. 27–36).

Wu, D., & Liang, S. (2018). Mobile search behaviors: An in-depth analysis based on contexts, APPs, and devices. *Synthesis Lectures on Information Concepts, Retrieval, and Services, 10*(2), i–159.

Zagermann, J., Pfeil, U., von Bauer, P., Fink, D., & Reiterer, H. (2020, April). "It's in my other hand!"—Studying the interplay of interaction techniques and multi-tablet activities. In *Proceedings of the 2020 CHI Conference on Human Factors in Computing Systems* (pp. 1–13).

2

THEORIES RELATING TO CROSS-DEVICE SEARCH

2.1 Exploratory Search Theory

A cross-device search is usually an exploratory search process because it requires multiple queries and sessions to fulfill a complex information need. This is consistent with the finding that search behaviors of mobile-to-desktop search differ significantly from desktop-to-desktop search in terms of both information exploration and sense-making (Han, Yue, & He, 2015). A previous study designed exploratory search tasks to be used in a cross-device search experiment (Han, He, Yue, & Brusilovsky, 2015). In the process of cross-device searches, users experienced a changing search state from uncertain to clear (Wu, Dong, Tang, & Capra, 2020), which corresponds to exploratory search. While searching for an unknown fact the first time, users are unsure what results they will see, which puts them at an uncertain state of search. When the users check the fact again on a different device, by contrast, it will be a quick search with a clear target in mind. Therefore, exploratory search is related to cross-device search, and we included theories and studies of exploratory search in the review.

2.1.1 Definition of Exploratory Search

Exploratory search is regarded as a loosely defined concept with a definition that evolves with the development of systems (Palagi, Gandon, Giboin, & Troncy, 2017). Marchionini (2006) took the first step of characterizing and conceptualizing exploratory search. Maslow's hierarchy of needs theory suggests that when their basic physiological needs are satisfied, people seek to fulfill higher levels of social and psychological needs. Similarly, searchers use different strategies and tactics to fulfill different levels of information need from basic to complex, which leads to the construction of different information-seeking activities. Marchionini

DOI: 10.4324/9780429201677-2

depicted three types of information-seeking activities (lookup, learn and investigate) and stressed that exploratory search is relevant to both learn and investigate activities. Exploratory search can be differentiated from lookup search according to two facets, goal and complexity, suggesting that exploratory search involves imprecise goals and a high degree of complexity (Athukorala, Głowacka, Jacucci, Oulasvirta, & Vreeken, 2016).

Cognitive activities are often highlighted when defining exploratory search. Defining a search as exploratory not only refers to the act of exploring, but also involves the complex cognitive activities associated with knowledge acquisition and the development of intellectual skills (White & Roth, 2009). Exploratory search can describe both information-seeking contexts and information-seeking processes. The former are characterized as open-ended, persistent, and multi-faceted, and the latter are depicted as opportunistic, iterative, and multi-tactical (Marchionini, 2006). To some extent, exploratory search is defined as a specialization of information exploration, where engaged people express a state of being uncertain about their goals, the domain of their goals, and the ways to achieve their goals (White & Roth, 2009). As suggested, exploratory search includes an abundance of behaviors beyond typical search behavior, such as exploration, uncertainty, creativity, knowledge discovery, and learning (Hendahewa & Shah, 2017).

2.1.2 Models of Exploratory Search

To conceptualize exploratory search, a framework of search characteristics has been proposed (Palagi et al., 2017). According to this, characteristics are clustered into three groups: (1) the characteristics about only the exploratory search, including: an open-ended search activity which can occur over time; an evolving information need; multi-faceted, several one-off pinpoint searches; and multiple possible answers; (2) characteristics about the user's inner state, including an anomalous state of knowledge and an ill-structured (vague, general or unsure) context of a search or goals, and a serendipitous attitude; (3) the characteristics which refer to both the search and the user, including fluctuating uncertainty, multiple targets/goals of a search, an evolving information need, and not expecting an exact answer.

Many information-seeking behavior models can be used to support and explain the exploratory search's points, such as exploration, uncertainty, and learning. Kuhlthau's Information Search Process (ISP) model (1991, 2004) describes six stages of information seeking to accomplish a goal from a user perspective, with regard to initiation, selection, exploration, formulation, collection, and presentation. Different types of search behavior are exhibited within each of these stages, and the exploration behavior in the model sheds light on exploratory search. Belkin's Anomalous State of Knowledge (ASK) model (Belkin, Oddy, & Brooks, 1982) suggests users' information needs generate from the uncertainty in their knowledge base, and explains how information-seeking behaviors change their initial state of knowledge. This theory explains uncertainty in exploratory search. Dervin's sense-making model regards information seeking as being a situation

12 Theories Relating to Cross-device Search

sensitive sense-making process (Dervin & Nilan, 1986). Users search in order to overcome the cognitive gap of attempting to make sense of observed data. This model can be used to make sense of learning in exploratory search.

Theories of information foraging and berry-picking are also relevant to exploratory search. Pirolli and Card's (1999) information foraging model connects food-foraging behaviors with information-seeking behaviors, explaining how searchers use information paths and cues (e.g., links and citations) to maximize their rate of gaining valuable information. Bate's (1989) berry-picking model compares the information-seeking process with the act of picking berries on bushes, discussing how search strategies shift as information is gathered during the search process. This model highlights the exploratory nature of information seeking, where every piece of information can inspire the searcher to refine the query and update the information need. It is possible to observe both information foraging and berry-picking behaviors in exploratory search. These two theoretical frameworks were compared in order to analyze the motivators for exploratory search and the nature of search processes (Savolainen, 2018). The berry-picking model considers changing information needs as the main drive and highlights focused searching as a critical constituent of exploratory search. The information-foraging theory stresses the need for performing a task as the primary trigger and focuses on exploratory browsing.

2.2 Successive Search Theory

Successive search is related to cross-device search, and refers to the process of repeated, successive searching over time. A cross-device search is comprised of at least two successive search sessions (i.e., a pre-switch session and post-switch session), and it is possible that repeated search activities occur between sessions. Moreover, the cross-device search is regarded as a particular case of cross-session search, and multi-/cross-session is one type of successive search. Therefore, theories related to successive searches were reviewed.

2.2.1 Spink's Theory of Successive Search

Amanda Spink is one of the first authors to be interested in studying the successive search phenomenon. She has contributed a series of explorations on successive search regarding definitions, characteristics and theoretical frameworks, which form Spink's theory of successive search.

Successive search is defined as the process of repeated, successive search sessions over time in relation to an evolving information problem, consisting of multiple successive search episodes. "Episode" is an alternative concept of search session referring to a user's interactions with the search system, which are divided by a time period (Spink, Bateman, & Griesdorf, 1998). The successive search phenomenon was firstly observed among end-users of online public access catalogs and CD-ROM databases (Spink, 1996). Results show 57% of end-users conduct multiple search sessions during their research project.

The successive search was also witnessed among web search users, and its reasons and characteristics were investigated (Spink, Griesdorf, & Bateman, 1999). It was found that information seekers engage in an average of two searches. In addition, many information seekers are engaging in three or more searches. The main reason for conducting successive searches is to refine or extend previous searches, where new databases are visited, and queries are changed. With the successive search processed, information seekers' understanding and evaluation of results evolve (Spink, Bateman, & Jansen, 1999).

An extension study based on this previous exploration proposes a framework of information-seeking approaches to successive searching (Spink, Wilson, Ford, Foster, & Ellis, 2002). The framework suggests that relevance may be understood as an impetus to successive searches. The evolution of the user's information problem is affected by the information found or not found, how the user defines relevance, and how that definition is applied in making relevance judgments.

2.2.2 Extension Theory of Successive Search

Spink used the term "multiple search sessions model" to indicate successive searches in her earliest study of this phenomenon (Spink, 1996). One model relevant to successive search was proposed using the name Multiple Information Seeking Episodes (MISE) (Lin & Belkin, 2000). Unfortunately, we were unable to access the full text of that paper, though a brief summary of the MISE model can be seen as follows:

> MISE consists of the four dimensions of information seeking experience: problematic situation, information problem, information seeking process, and episode. A problematic situation is the users' subjective perception and estimate of carrying out a goal with their existing knowledge in the objective context. An information problem is the result of that perception and estimate, requiring external information to explicate. The explication of information problem is manifested as the information seeking process, constituted by the activities users engage in when interacting with information resources for information seeking. The time period between the initiation and termination of interacting with a particular external information resource is the episode.
>
> *(Lin 2001)*

The MISE model was further updated by identifying eight modes of multiple information-seeking episodes, as well as properties of the mentioned four dimensions. Eight different modes of MISE were concluded on the basis of eight reasons for the renewal of successive information seeking, consisting of: transmuting, spawning, transiting, rolling back, unanswered, lost-treatment, cultivated, and anticipated (Lin & Belkin, 2005). The updated MISE model involves more factors of both user and system aspects, shifting from user-centered to interaction-centered. An empirical study of the MISE model's renewal demonstrates how

14 Theories Relating to Cross-device Search

critical factors in the information-seeking process evolve over sessions and how those factors are affected by other factors (Lin, 2005). It was also found that the searchers' level of subject knowledge significantly improves over the sessions.

Another extended theory based on successive search lies in conceptualizing search genres (Bowler, 2009). This study found that the search process consists of a many-to-many relationship, with several search genres embedded within the process, representing different information needs. The search genres concept, lying somewhere between successive search (single topic) and multitasking search (multiple topics), can be used to map irregularities in successive searching. For example, search genres can describe a situation where a user looks for multiple topics simultaneously and the searches circle around a high-level information problem.

2.3 Theoretical Models Supporting Cross-device Search Research

An increasing number of studies have been interested in cross-device search. Although theories concentrating on cross-device search tend to be rare, there are existing theoretical models relevant to cross-device interaction or cross-device computing. These theoretical models were reviewed to determine how they can support cross-device search research.

2.3.1 Cross-device Taxonomy

Cross-device taxonomy is a unified taxonomy for the emerging domain of cross-device computing, which is proposed based on the analysis of 510 papers in the corresponding domain. The taxonomy consists of six aspects: the ontology of cross-device research terminology, the taxonomy of key characteristics of the cross-device design space, cross-device application domains, the classification of tracking systems for cross-device interfaces, cross-device interaction techniques, and evaluation strategies for cross-device work (Brudy, 2020; Brudy, Holz, Rädle, Wu, & Marquardt, 2019).

One part of the ontology of cross-device research terminology presents diverse terms related to "cross-device" and sorts out the nested relationship of terms. The other part demonstrates a list of keywords describing the research focus, including interaction/collaboration, (user) interfaces, applications/systems, platform/middleware, environments/ecologies and computing. Through the terminology ontology, the areas of cross-device research and its evolution are clear. The earliest cross-device research began from the observation of personal workstations; therefore, the terms "multi-monitor/screen" and "dual-display/monitor" emerge. These terms construct the bottom level of the ontology, which extends to an upper level with the terms "cross-display" and "multi-display." Among studies using "cross-display" and "multi-display," more types of computing devices are involved, such as digital wall displays, interactive whiteboards and television sets. Meanwhile, due to the occurrence of these large interfaces, terms further extend to "cross-surface," "multi-surface" and "trans-surface." With the development of mobile devices (e.g. smartphones, tablets, wearable devices, smart glasses, etc.), the terms "multi-slate/tablet" and "multi-mobile" are utilized. To unify cross-device terminology, these various terms are grouped into "cross-device," "multi-device" and "distributed," which form the top level of the ontology.

The taxonomy of key characteristics of the cross-device design space examines the following six dimensions of cross-device interaction. (1) The temporal dimension indicates whether interactions happen synchronously or asynchronously. (2) The configuration dimension refers the setup of cross-device systems. Synchronous cross-device interaction could involve mirroring the same content on multiple displays (mirrored), or spatially or logically distributed interfaces (distributed). Asynchronous cross-device interaction could involve migratory interfaces or cross-platform applications. (3) The relationship dimension classifies cross-device interaction situations according to a single user/device or multiple users/devices involved. (4) The scale dimension describes the reachable distance between users and devices. (5) The dynamics dimension demonstrates the flexibility of cross-device interaction spaces, including fixed, semi-fixed and mobile. (6) The space dimension differentiates between co-located and remoted cross-device interactions.

Cross-device application domains identify the following nine categories: knowledge work, home computing, data exploration, mobile computing, games/installations, collaboration, education, health, and software development. Tracking systems for cross-device interfaces are classified in terms of tracking characteristics (proximity vs. relative location vs. 2D vs. 3D) and modalities (capacitive, inertial, acoustic, magnetic, optical, and audio). Interaction techniques for cross-device computing has experienced three phases, and the input modalities can be grouped into on-screen interaction, interaction and gestures around the device, device motion, changing the shape of the devices, and using body gestures.

The classification of evaluation strategies in the cross-device domain falls into five methods: informative studies (cross-device users' needs), evaluation through demonstration (what a cross-device system/technique can do), evaluation through usage (the usability and usefulness of a cross-device system/technique), technical evaluation (performance of a cross-device system/technique), and heuristic evaluation (usability assessment by metrics).

2.3.2 INFEX Framework

In an ideal situation, end-users of cross-device interactions should be allowed to share information across any device, regardless of hardware, interfaces or systems. Unfortunately, in reality, the applications and practices of cross-device interaction are limited by a few types of devices (e.g., laptops, smartphones, tablets), inconsistent communication protocols (e.g., WiFi-based connection or Bluetooth) and specific types of media (e.g., cross-device photo sharing). With more devices being included in cross-device design, user experience is at risk due to the way users operate and interact with the devices. Therefore, a unifying framework for cross-device usage, INFEX, is proposed to help end-users exchange and explore information easily across heterogeneous devices, and to help cross-device product developers break the restrictions of hardware or protocols (Roels, Witte, & Signer, 2017).

The architecture of the INFEX framework consists of three components. First, a fundamental component is the plug-ins for detecting devices that the user wants to include in the interaction. Different mechanisms can be used to specify the participating device; for example, placing the device on an interactive interface, or selecting the device in a GUI (Graphical User Interface). Second, it is important to have a component to mediate devices with different communication protocols. Various communication plug-ins are implemented in the INFEX framework to process different protocols. For example, INFEX, acting as a mediator, searches for a photo via WiFi from the camera, and then sends it to the printer via Bluetooth. Third, the GUI component of INFEX can capture user input and provide users with an interactive interface for listing, inspecting, and transferring device content. These three components are tied together through the core logic of INFEX.

The INFEX framework designs an architecture for transferring information across heterogeneous devices, and is hardware and protocol independent, since more detection and communication plug-ins could be added to handle existing and emerging devices and protocols. Thus, developers who are going to use the INFEX framework can create their own highly customized cross-device products.

2.3.3 Cross-device Search Pattern Model

As introduced above, the cross-device taxonomy and INFEX framework both present theories about cross-device interaction/computing, while the model in this section specifically focuses on cross-device search.

Han, Yue, and He (2015) identified cross-device search patterns based on the Hidden Markov Model (HMM). HMM argues that observable actions are driven by a sequence of hidden states which forms a Markov chain. Each hidden state can transfer to, or be transferred from, another hidden state with different probabilities. In Han's cross-device search pattern model (Han, 2017), search patterns are assumed to be the hidden states that drive the user's cross-device search behaviors.

In Han's model, a cross-device search consists of the initial session and the continued session. The initial session includes three hidden states: labelled querying, exploration and exploitation, respectively. Querying is associated with the actions of issuing and repeating a query. Exploration is associated with short-dwell clicks, indicating the state of obtaining non-relevant documents, whereas exploitation is associated with long-dwell clicks and is the dominant state for relevant documents. Each state can transition to another with a certain probability.

On the other hand, compared with the initial session, the continued session includes an additional hidden state called re-finding. Re-finding refers the state of resuming the search task. In the continued session, the querying and re-finding states are more likely to occur at the beginning. Probabilities of transitions between the querying, exploration, and exploitation states indicate that users in the continued session tend to be more selective for relevant documents.

2.4 Summary

This chapter mainly discusses theories and theoretical models related to the cross-device search, aiming to understand cross-device search behavior through a theoretical point of view.

Theories and conceptual models related to exploratory search, successive search, and multi-session search are reviewed. A cross-device search is usually an exploratory search process because it requires multiple queries and sessions to complete a complex information need. Successive search is also related to cross-device search, and refers to the process of repeated, successive searching over time. A cross-device search is comprised of at least two successive search sessions (i.e., a pre-switch session and post-switch session), and it is possible that repeated search activities occur between sessions. Multi-session search has a clear relation to cross-device search, for it is regarded as a particular case of cross-session search.

Meanwhile, this chapter reviews the theoretical models of cross-device interaction and computing, as well as the HMM-based model of cross-device search patterns. The cross-device taxonomy characterizes cross-device computing in terms of cross-device research terminology, key characteristics of the cross-device design space, cross-device application domains, tracking systems for cross-device interfaces, cross-device interaction techniques, and evaluation strategies for cross-device work. The INFEX framework provides a solution to exchange and explore information easily across heterogeneous devices, regardless of the restriction of hardware or protocols. The cross-device search pattern model focuses on search activity across mobile and desktop devices, and identifies different search patterns in the initial and continued sessions.

Reference

Athukorala, K., Głowacka, D., Jacucci, G., Oulasvirta, A., & Vreeken, J. (2016). Is exploratory search different? A comparison of information search behavior for exploratory and lookup tasks. *Journal of the Association for Information Science & Technology, 67,* 2635–2651. doi:10.1002/asi.23617.

Bates, M. J. (1989). The design of browsing and berrypicking techniques for the online search interface. *Online Review, 13*(5), 407–424. doi:10.1108/eb024320.

Belkin, N., Oddy, R., & Brooks, H. (1982). Ask for information retrieval: Part 1. background and theory. *Journal of Documentation, 38*(2), 61–7. doi:10.1108/eb026722.

Bowler, L. (2009). Genres of search: A concept for understanding successive search behaviour. *Canadian Journal of Library and Information Science, 33*(3/4), 119–140.

Brudy, F. (2020). Designing for Cross-Device Interactions (Doctoral Thesis). University College London.

Brudy, F., Holz, C., Rädle, R., Wu, C. J., & Marquardt, N. (2019). Cross-device taxonomy: Survey, opportunities and challenges of interactions spanning across multiple devices. In *Proceedings of the 2019 CHI Conference on Human Factors in Computing Systems* (pp. 1–28). doi:10.1145/3290605.3300792.

Dervin, B., & Nilan, M. (1986). Information needs and uses. *Annual Review of Information Systems and Technology, 21*, 3–33.

Han, S. (2017). Understanding, modeling and supporting cross-device (Doctoral Thesis). University of Pittsburgh.

Han, S., He, D., Yue, Z., & Brusilovsky, P. (2015). Supporting cross-device web search with social navigation-based mobile touch interactions. In *Proceedings of the International Conference on user Modeling, Adaptation And Personalization* (pp. 143–155). doi:10.1007/978-3-319-20267-9_12

Han, S., Yue, Z., & He, D. (2015). Understanding and supporting cross-device web search for exploratory tasks with mobile touch interactions. *ACM Transactions on Information Systems, 33*(4), 1–34. doi:10.1145/2738036

Hendahewa, C., & Shah, C. (2017). Evaluating user search trails in exploratory search tasks. *Information Processing & Management, 53*(4), 905–922. doi:10.1016/j.ipm.2017.04.001.

Kuhlthau, C. C. (1991). Inside the search process: Information seeking from the user's perspective. *Journal of the American Society for Information Science, 42*(5), 361–371. doi:10.1002/(SICI)1097-4571(199106)42:5-361::AID-ASI6>3.0.CO;2-#.

Kuhlthau, C.C. (2004). *Seeking meaning: A Process approach to library and information services.* Michigan: Libraries Unlimited.

Lin, S. J. (2001). Understanding successive searches across multiple sessions over the web. *ICIS 2001 Proceedings* (pp. 531–536). https://aisel.aisnet.org/icis2001/67

Lin, S. J. (2005). Internetworking of factors affecting successive searches over multiple episodes. *Journal of the American Society for Information Science and Technology, 56*(4), 416–436. doi:10.1002/asi.20128

Lin, S. J., & Belkin, N. J. (2000). Modeling multiple information seeking episodes. *Proceedings of the 63rd Annual Meeting of the American Society for Information Science* (pp. 133–147).

Lin, S. J., & Belkin, N. J. (2005). Validation of a model of information seeking over multiple search sessions. *Journal of the American Society for Information Science and Technology, 56*(4), 393–415. doi:10.1002/asi.20127

Marchionini, G. (2006). Exploratory search: From finding to understanding. *Communication ACM, 49*(4), 41–46. doi:10.1145/1121949.1121979

Palagi, E., Gandon F., Giboin, A., & Troncy, R. (2017). A survey of definitions and models of exploratory search. In *Proceedings of the 2017 ACM Workshop on Exploratory Search and Interactive Data Analytics* (pp. 3–8). doi:10.1145/3038462.3038465

Pirolli, P., & Card, S. (1999). Information foraging. *Psychological Review, 106*(4), 643–675. doi:10.1037/0033-295X.106.4.643

Roels, R., Witte, A. D., & Signer, B. (2017). INFEX: A unifying framework for cross-device information exploration and exchange. *Proceedings of the ACM on Human-Computer Interaction, 2*, 1–26). doi:10.1145/3179427.

Savolainen, R. (2018). Berrypicking and information foraging: Comparison of two theoretical frameworks for studying exploratory search. *Journal of Information Science, 44*(5), 580–593. doi:10.1177/0165551517713168

Spink, A. (1996), Multiple search sessions model of end-user behavior: An exploratory study. *Journal of the Association for Information Science & Technology, 47*, 603–609. doi:10.1002/(SICI)1097-4571(199608)47:8<603::AID-ASI4>3.0.CO;2-X

Spink, A., Bateman, J., & Griesdorf, H. (1998). Successive searching behavior during information retrieval (IR): Development of a new line of research. In *Proceedings of the 26th Annual Meeting of the Canadian Association for Information Science* (pp. 401–415).

Spink, A., Bateman, J., & Jansen, B. J. (1999). Searching the Web: A survey of EXCITE users. *Internet Research, 9*(2), 117–128. doi:10.1108/10662249910264882

Spink, A., Griesdorf, H., & Bateman, J. (1999). A study of mediated successive searching during information seeking. *Journal of Information Science, 25*(6), 477–487. doi:10.1177/016555159902500604

Spink, A., Wilson, T., Ford, N., Foster, A., & Ellis, D. (2002), Information seeking and mediated searching study. Part 3. Successive searching. *Journal of the Association for Information Science & Technology, 53,* 716–727. doi:10.1002/asi.10083

White, R. W., & Roth, R. A. (2009). Exploratory search: Beyond the query-response paradigm. *Synthesis Lectures on Information Concepts, Retrieval, and Services, 1*(1), 1–98. doi:10.2200/S00174ED1V01Y200901ICR003

Wu, D., Dong, J., Tang, Y., & Capra, R. (2020). Understanding task preparation and resumption behaviors in cross-device search. *Journal of the Association for Information Science and Technology, 71,* 887–901. doi:10.1002/asi.24307

3

CROSS-DEVICE SEARCH TOPICS

3.1 Existing Exploration on Cross-Device Search Topics

A user's information need plays an essential role in understanding information-seeking behavior. In a famous paper, *The Process of Asking Questions* (1962), Taylor explains the concept of information need by discussing how an individual asks a question and receives an answer from an information system. Four levels of information need are summarized through the process of question formation. According to Taylor, information needs are looked upon as the description of an area of doubt. It is difficult to assign a comprehensive and accurate definition of such an abstract concept, though we are able to gain insight through search tasks.

Merriam-Webster Dictionary defines topic as "the subject of a discourse or of a section of a discourse." The analysis of search topics is usually accompanied by research on search tasks (Hienert, Mitsui, Mayr, Shah, & Belkin, 2018). The issue of task identification can be transferred to a topic identification problem (Li, Deng, He, Dong, Chang, & Zha, 2016). Ozmutlu (2006) proposed an automatic method of task identification using multiple linear regression based on the statistical relationship between query characteristics and topic shift and continuation. To some extent, the term topic is used to describe a task. In information retrieval evaluation campaigns like TREC, "topic" is used to describe a scenario for concrete information seeking, which is represented by task type and subject. Similarly, "topic" in this chapter is a broad term similar to the concept of task. We reviewed the existing exploration of cross-device search topics, specifically the subjects, task types, and task complexity.

DOI: 10.4324/9780429201677-3

3.1.1 Subjects in Cross-device Search

There is considerable existing research on topic classification, exploring what subjects of information users search. Wang, Huang, & White (2013) led in studying subject characteristics of cross-device search, specifically the sustainability of query subjects during device switching. According to their findings, the most sustainable topics across devices are image, navigational, book, celebrities, and music. In their study, researchers only considered the device switch; namely, whether the search device changed, rather than what the exact devices were. Montañez, White, & Huang (2014) presented subject distributions on four specific device types and found a probability gap of certain subjects between the current and previous devices, which indicates subject characteristics of the cross-device search. Contrasting the above discussion of cross-device searching on web searches, Wu, Liang, & Bi (2018) investigated cross-device OPAC searches. Results show that OPAC users mainly issue queries about industry and technology, literature, history, geography, and economics between desktop and mobile devices.

Although research on cross-device search subjects has emerged in recent years, general web search subjects have been well studied for some time. Jansen, Liu, Weaver, Campbell, & Gregg (2011) used transaction logs with a real-time search engine and classified queries into subject categories. According to their findings, the leading subject categories for which users frequently searched are society, arts, and computers. This differs from the findings of studies on traditional web searches. According to Beitzel, Jensen, Chowdhury, Grossman, & Frieder (2004), the three most retrieved subjects are shopping, entertainment, and pornography. Chau, Fang, & Sheng (2005) found that the search subjects of website search engine users differ considerably from those of general search engine users. Differences in information needs are a possible reason for this. In addition to the context of web searches, academic database query subjects have also been investigated (Liang & Leng, 2020).

3.1.2 Task Type

A number of studies have examined task type in search task research. Various search task classification schemes have been proposed based on different facets of the search task. Li and Belkin (2008) thoroughly reviewed these classification schemes, concluding that such schemes would include characteristics of the product of the search, the source of the task, and the complexity of the task. They constructed a comprehensive classification scheme that took into account multiple facets (see Table 3.1). These facets represent different aspects of the task, explaining (1) Where is this task from? (2) Who carries it out? (3) How long does this task last? (4) What is it about (topic or content)? (5) How should this task be completed? (6) What is (are) its product(s)? and (7) What is (are) its goal(s)?

Task type as a contextual factor has been given a great deal of attention in studies about information-seeking behavior. Researchers have investigated how different task types impact users' search behaviors. Referring to the multi-facet

22 Cross-device Search Topics

TABLE 3.1 Faceted classification of tasks (Li & Belkin, 2008) (WT refers to Work Task, ST refers to Search Task)

	Facet	*Sub-Facet*	*Value*
Generic facet of task	Source of task	(N/A)	Internal generated
			Collaboration
			External assigned
	Task doer	(N/A)	Individual
			Individual in a group
			Group
	Time	Frequency	Unique
			Intermittent
			Routine
		Length	Short-term
			Long-term
		Stage	Beginning
			Middle
			Final
	Product	(N/A)	Physical (for WT)
			Intellectual (for WT and ST)
			Decision/Solution (for WT)
			Factual information (for ST)
			Image (for ST)
			Mix product (for ST)
	Process	(N/A)	One-time task
			Multi-time task
	Goal	Quality	Specific goal
			Amorphous goal
			Mixed goal
		Quantity	Multi-goal
			Single-goal
Common attributes of task	Task characteristics	Objective task complexity	High complexity
			Moderate
			Low complexity
		Interdependence	High interdependence
			Moderate
			Low interdependence
	User's perception of task	Salience of a task	High salience
			Moderate
			Low salience
		Urgency	Immediate (urgent)
			Moderate
			Delayed (not urgent)
		Difficulty	High difficulty
			Moderate
			Low difficulty
		Subjective task complexity	High complexity
			Moderate
			Low complexity
		Knowledge of task topic	High knowledge
			Moderate
			Low knowledge
		Knowledge of task procedure	High knowledge
			Moderate
			Low knowledge

classification scheme, Liu, Liu, & Belkin (2013) used four tasks – facets of task product, level, task goal, and complexity – and examined users' behaviors in the different task types. Liu, Gwizdka, Liu, & Belkin (2010) found that user behaviors on the whole-session and within-session levels predict task difficulty in terms of fact-finding tasks and information-gathering tasks. These task types were created by Kellar, Watters, & Shepherd (2007).

3.1.3 Task Complexity Measurement

Many researchers are interested in task complexity and difficulty, two terms that have been used ambiguously. Task difficulty is defined as the user's perception of task complexity (Kim, 2006). It has been suggested that task difficulty is a subjective measure, whereas task complexity can be either objective or subjective (Gwizdka & Spence, 2006). Previous studies have proposed many ways of measuring task complexity. The objective aspect of task complexity is represented by task characteristics; for example, the word count of a task description (Li et al., 2011) and the number of subtasks (Li & Belkin, 2010). The subjective aspect of task complexity is associated with users' cognition and information needs. An influential study by Campbell (1988) identified contributors of task complexity, which are related to the user's desire and state. Knowing what makes a task complex can help in measuring task complexity. Mosenthal (1998) proposed an evaluation framework for task complexity consisting of three dimensions: type of information requested, type of match, and plausibility of distractors. Byström & Järvelin (1995) utilized a complexity categorization based on characteristics relating to the a priori determinability of tasks, which involves repetition, analyzability, a priori determinability, the number of alternative paths of task performance, and outcome novelty. They constructed the relationships of task complexity, necessary information types, information channels, and sources. Vakkari & Kuokkanen (1997) further reconstructed the theoretical structure of these relationships.

In this chapter, we measure topic complexity by referring to the measurement of task complexity. The measurement of topic complexity used in this chapter is the same as that utilized by Wildemuth, Kelly, Boettcher, Moore, & Dimitrova (2018). They classified levels of task complexity from a cognitive perspective, using a revised framework of Bloom's Taxonomy proposed by Krathwohl (2002).

According to this revised framework (see Table 3.2), the complexity of the knowledge dimension increases along the sequence of factual knowledge, conceptual knowledge, procedural knowledge, and metacognitive knowledge. Factual knowledge refers to the basic elements that individuals must know in order to be acquainted with a discipline or solve problems within it; terminology is one example. Conceptual knowledge is explained as interrelationships among the basic elements within a larger structure that enable them to function together, such as classifications and categories, theories, and models. Procedural knowledge indicates how to do something, such as methods of inquiry and criteria for using techniques. Metacognitive knowledge is the knowledge of cognition; for instance,

24 Cross-device Search Topics

TABLE 3.2 Revised framework of Bloom's Taxonomy (Krathwohl, 2002)

		Cognitive process dimension					
		Remember	*Understand*	*Apply*	*Analyze*	*Evaluate*	*Create*
Knowledge dimension	Factual knowledge	☐	☐	☐	☐	☐	☐
	Conceptual knowledge	☐	☐	☐	☐	☐	☐
	Procedural knowledge	☐	☐	☐	☐	☐	☐
	Metacognitive knowledge	☐	☐	☐	☐	☐	☐

strategic knowledge, contextual and conditional knowledge, and self-knowledge. The complexity of the cognitive dimension increases through the cognitive process of information: remember, understand, apply, analyze, evaluate, and create.

3.2 Crowdsourcing Survey on Cross-device Search Topics

3.2.1 Motivation

We aim to explore the characteristics of cross-device search topics in order to further understand cross-device search information needs, which is fundamental to improving designs for search engines and search functions in applications. Similar to TREC, "topic" in this chapter is deemed a broad term similar to the concept of task. The first step in analyzing cross-device search topics is extracting them in authentic situations. One method of data collection is transaction logs. In log analysis, the search task refers to a set of queries successively submitted during a limited period. Each period indicates a search session identified using a timeout. If the user stops querying beyond a certain time, the search session is over. This method extracts search tasks based on search sessions. Wang et al. (2013) utilized this method to identify cross-device search tasks. Two adjacent sessions that occur on different devices constitute a cross-device search task. One shortcoming of this method is that the topics of the two sessions might be distinct.

Another way to collect data on authentic cross-device search tasks is self-reporting by users, a method that was used in this chapter. Users described their own experiences of a cross-device search, and the content of the description was analyzed. Compared with transaction logs, descriptions by users themselves can reflect more contextual factors of search topics, which helps to better interpret the users' information needs. For the generalizability of findings and to ensure population variety, crowdsourcing was used.

3.2.2 Crowdsourcing Platforms

We collected cross-device search descriptions through a crowdsourcing survey. Crowdsourcing is an emerging concept that describes an online problem-solving activity in the form of an open call. Howe (2006) indicates that crowdsourcing

Cross-device Search Topics **25**

is an action of a company or institution. Estellés-Arolas & González-Ladrón-de-Guevara (2012) expand the initiator of crowdsourcing to include individuals. The initiator publishes a task online and it is distributed to participants of interest, which means that a group of participants with a variety of backgrounds can be involved. In previous surveys, participants are often university students or employees of a certain company, and this limits the generalizability of findings due to their limited experiences. This is why we use crowdsourcing for the current survey.

Moreover, to increase the variety of participants, foreigners, as well as Chinese users, were considered. Amazon Mechanical Turk is a well-known crowdsourcing platform, and we used it to target the survey at individuals around the globe. Kittur, Chi, & Suh (2008) verified the utility of Amazon Mechanical Turk in user studies. It is a useful way to collect bona fide answers at a low cost rather than gathering inferior responses. The survey was only distributed to Master Workers identified as high-performing workers on Amazon Mechanical Turk. Each valid response was rewarded with one dollar. Because Chinese users of Amazon Mechanical Turk are rare, we investigated Chinese users through Baidu Crowd Test and Wen Juan Xing, two crowdsourcing platforms in China. We published the survey on Baidu Crowd Test first, and the number of valid responses did not meet our expectations. Thus, we attempted to increase the number with the help of Wen Juan Xing. It is not necessary to worry about overlapping respondents between the two platforms due to the million-level user base. Valid respondents were paid with coupons.

3.2.3 Survey Design

The questionnaire is in two parts and can be seen in Table 3.3. Part one (Q1–13) covers the description and details of a recent cross-device search experience, and part two (Q14–18) covers the demographics of participants.

TABLE 3.3 Cross-device search experience survey

Part One (Q1–13)

---

1. Have you ever successively searched for the same topic using two different devices (i.e. cross-device search)?

◯ yes
◯ no (survey ends)

2. Please recall and describe in detail your latest experience of cross-device search.

_____

Some tips to help you recall: When and where did you perform the cross-device search? What did you search for? How did you perform the search?

3. According to your cross-device search experience described above, which search device did you use before you switched device?

◯ smartphone
◯ tablet/iPad
◯ laptop
◯ desktop
◯ other device _____

26 Cross-device Search Topics

4. According to your cross-device search experience described above, which search device did you use after you switched device?
○ smartphone
○ tablet/iPad
○ laptop
○ desktop
○ other device _____

5. According to your cross-device search experience described above, how many queries did you submit using the pre-switch search device?
○ 1–2
○ 3–4
○ 5–6
○ more than 6
☐

6. According to your cross-device search experience described above, how many queries did you submit using the post-switch search device?
○ 1–2
○ 3–4
○ 5–6
○ more than 6
☐

7. According to your cross-device search experience described above, how many pages did you visit using the pre-switch search device?
○ 1–5
○ 6–10
○ 11–15
○ more than 15
☐

8. According to your cross-device search experience described above, how many pages did you visit using the post-switch search device?
○ 1–5
○ 6–10
○ 11–15
○ more than 15
☐

9. According to your cross-device search experience described above, how long was the interval between the searches on the two devices?
○ hour(s) _____ ★ (Please firstly choose hour/minute as the unit, then write the number)
○ minute(s) _____ ★ (Please firstly choose hour/minute as the unit, then write the number)
☐

Cross-device Search Topics 27

10. According to your cross-device search experience described above, why did you switch the device to resume the same topic?

○ A planned cross-device search. (*I knew I would search for the topic on more than one device.*)

○ Unsatisfied information need. (*I didn't find what I wanted on the pre-switch device.*)

○ Helping memory. (*I forgot what I searched for on the pre-switch device, so I wanted to search for it again.*)

○ Forced to interrupt the search. (*Because of an unknown interruption, I had to stop the current search and resumed it on another device.*)

○ Complement existing search results. (*Even though I got what I wanted on the pre-switch search device, I expected to acquire more useful information by switching search device.*)

○ Other reasons _____

☐

11. According to your cross-device search experience described above, what task type do you think it is?

○ Factual (*specific question and specific answer, e.g. you want to visit the oldest restaurant in town and you search for the name of the restaurant.*)

○ Interpretive (*specific question and general answer, e.g. you want to know the effects of smoking and you search for what could happen to smokers.*)

○ Exploratory (*general question and general answer, e.g. you come across a new thing [for example, artificial intelligence] and you want to learn about it.*)

☐

12. According to your cross-device search experience described above, please judge the task complexity of the search from the knowledge dimension.

○ Factual knowledge (*The basic elements that people must know to be acquainted with a discipline or solve problems in it [e.g. terminology, specific details]*).

○ Conceptual knowledge (*The interrelationships between the basic elements within a larger structure that enable them to function together [e.g. classifications and categories, principles and generalizations, theories, models, and structures]*).

○ Procedural knowledge (*How to do something; methods of inquiry, and criteria for using skills, algorithms, techniques, and methods*).

○ Metacognitive knowledge (*Knowledge of cognition in general as well as awareness and knowledge of one's own cognition [e.g. strategic knowledge, contextual and conditional knowledge, self-knowledge]*).

☐

13. According to your cross-device search experience described above, please judge the task complexity of the search from the cognitive dimension.

The cognitive process of information develops as: remember → understand → apply → analyze → evaluate → create

○ remember
○ understand
○ apply
○ analyze
○ evaluate
○ create

28 Cross-device Search Topics

Part Two (14–18)

---

14. What is your gender?
○ male
○ female
☐

15. What is your age?
○ younger than 18
○ 18–25
○ 26–30
○ 31–35
○ 36–40
○ older than 40
☐

16. What is your highest degree of education?
○ elementary school and below
○ junior high school and equivalent
○ high school and equivalent
○ bachelor and equivalent
○ master and above
☐

17. What is your current job?
○ working in government offices
○ working in a company
○ working at a school
○ student
○ self-employed
○ other _____
☐

18. What is your nationality?

Q1 is a filtering question. Only those who claim to have ever had cross-device search experience can see the rest of the survey. Q2 is the core of the survey. It asks participants to describe one cross-device search in as much detail as possible. Unavoidably, the thoroughness of the description varies from person to person.

Q3–13 are used to supplement details. Q3 and Q4 ask for details about the search device before and after the device switch. The options provide commonly used mobile and desktop search devices, namely smartphone, tablet/iPad, desktop computer, and laptop computer. Q5–8 investigate the number of queries issued and pages/apps visited before and after the device switch. The options make reference to the study by Liu et al. (2010). They recruited 48 university students to complete 12 search tasks that varied in difficulty and found the maximum mean number of queries was 6.24 and the corresponding number of viewed pages was 15.39. Q9 checks the length of time between switching devices. In previous studies, the interval threshold to identify a cross-device search task has been inconsistent. Wang et al. (2013) set a six-hour limit to exclude long-term device-switching, which covers 50% of switches in their logs. Montañez et al. (2014) used a three-hour threshold in order to improve the likelihood of extracting meaningful cross-device transitions. We intend to shed light on the interval of switches in a real situation. Q10 surveys the driving force of searching across different devices, which reveals the demand for device-switching (RQ2(c)). The reasons listed as options are concluded based on our previous study of a cross-device search experiment (Wu, Dong, & Tang, 2018).

Q11–13 require participants to classify the task type and complexity of the cross-device search described. For the validity of results and to help respondents understand, we have provided explanations and examples for each option in Q11–13. Task types include factual tasks, interpretive tasks, and exploratory tasks, which differ by specificity of question and answer (Kim, 2006). The complexity of cross-device searching was judged on two dimensions, knowledge and cognition, according to the revised framework of Bloom's Taxonomy (Krathwohl, 2002). The cognition dimension of the framework was also used in the study by Wildemuth et al. (2018) to assess task complexity. As we assume the information need is multi-dimensional, the complexity of needs shown by the task complexity should also be evaluated from more than one dimension. The knowledge dimension of the framework measures the complexity of the information content, while the cognition dimension measures the complexity of understanding of the information.

Q14–18 collect information on the background of participants in terms of gender, age, education, career, and nationality.

3.2.4 Respondent Backgrounds

The crowdsourcing survey lasted from November 2, 2018 to December 25, 2018. We received 158, 203, and 106 replies from Amazon Mechanical Turk, Baidu Crowd Test, and Wen Juan Xing, respectively. There were 124 invalid replies, where, for example, the description was not about a specific cross-device search, devices were the same before and after the device switch, or the device-switching interval was 0 minutes. In total, we obtained 343 valid replies (139 from Amazon Mechanical Turk, 101 from Baidu Crowd Test and 103 from Wen Juan Xing). The participants' demographics can be seen in Table 3.4. The numbers of male and female respondents were relatively well balanced. Respondents were spread across all ages, with levels of education concentrated in bachelor and equivalent. Office workers predominated among all respondents, and almost all respondents were Chinese and American.

3.3 Cross-Device Search Topic Identification

3.3.1 Coding Topic Features

To identify features of cross-device search topics, we conducted a content analysis of descriptions and answers from the survey results. Two coders were involved in

30 Cross-device Search Topics

TABLE 3.4 Demographics of participants

Gender	Male	185
	Female	158
Age	<18	4
	18–25	76
	26–30	84
	31–35	76
	36–40	53
	>40	50
Education	Junior high school or equivalent	2
	High school or equivalent	58
	Bachelor's or equivalent	245
	Master's or above	38
Career	Working in government offices	19
	Working in a company	201
	Working in a school	25
	Students	37
	Self-employed	56
	Other	5
Nationality	China (204), USA (123), India (12), UK (2), Iceland (1), Serbia (1)	

two rounds of coding. Both coders major in Library and Information Science and are equipped with good reading skills in English.

The initial coding scheme was based on the Multiple Information Seeking Episodes (MISE) model (Lin & Belkin, 2005). The MISE model explains why and how people engage in multiple information-seeking episodes, which fits the cross-device search. The model has four dimensions: problematic situation, information-seeking process, information problem, and episodes. Each dimension is characterized by a set of properties. The initial coding scheme included these properties as categories. Thirty samples (15 from Amazon Mechanical Turk, and 15 from Baidu Crowd Test and Wen Juan Xing) selected by random sampling were used for coding training, with the initial coding scheme revised according to characteristics of the survey results. The revised coding scheme is shown in Table 3.5. Four dimensions based on the MISE model are included, each consisting of different categories and types. Coding sources for each category and type are noted.

For the first round of coding, two coders coded the content of the 343 valid replies together and discussed any points of disagreement in order to ensure coding reliability. For the second round of coding, coders further coded the *Goal, Subject,* and *Outcome* of the cross-device search tasks. Coding reliability was examined by calculating Scott's pi (Scott, 1955). This measure was selected because the coded content was a large sample, only nominal data, and coded by two coders (Wildemuth, 2017, p. 311). The overall Scott's pi was 0.98, with no

Cross-device Search Topics **31**

TABLE 3.5 Coding scheme

Dimension	Category	Definition	Type	Source
Information Problem	Subject	Subject categories that users search for	(2nd round coding)	Q2
	Type	Specific and general degree of task	Factual Interpretive Exploratory	Q11
	Complexity of Knowledge Dimension	Complexity of task from knowledge and cognitive dimensions	Factual knowledge Conceptual knowledge Procedural knowledge Metacognitive knowledge	Q12
	Complexity of Cognitive Dimension		Remember Understand Apply Analyze Evaluate Create	Q13
Information-Seeking Process	Pre-switch Device	Equipment used to search before switching	Smartphone Tablet/iPad Laptop Desktop	Q3
	Post-switch Device	Equipment used to search after switching	Smartphone Tablet/iPad Laptop Desktop	Q4
	Search System	Search engines/ applications used for search	Baidu Google Others	Q2
	Issued Query	Terms submitted to search	N/A	Q2, Q5, & Q6
	Visited Page	Number of pages the user visited	N/A	Q7 & Q8
	Outcome	Discussion at the end of the search	(2nd round coding)	Q2
Problematic Situation	Goal	Purpose of search	(2nd round coding)	Q2
	Environment	Whether place changes during the search	Changed place Unchanged place	Q2 Q2

(*Continued*)

32 Cross-device Search Topics

TABLE 3.5 (Continued)

Dimension	Category	Definition	Type	Source
Episodes	Device Switch	Direction of switching devices	Smartphone to tablet/ iPad	Q3 & Q4
			Smartphone to laptop	
			Smartphone to desktop	
			Tablet/iPad to smartphone	
			Tablet/iPad to laptop	
			Tablet/iPad to desktop	
			Laptop to smartphone	
			Laptop to tablet/iPad	
			Laptop to desktop	
			Desktop to smartphone	
			Desktop to tablet/iPad	
			Desktop to laptop	
	Switching Interval	Time it takes to switch devices	Within an hour	Q9
			Over an hour	
	Switching Reasons	Reasons for switching devices to resume the search	Planned cross-device search	Q2 & Q10
			Unsatisfied information need	
			Helping memory	
			Forced to interrupt the search	
			Complementing existing search results	
			Others	

category achieving lower than 0.95. It is generally agreed that a measure of coding agreement above 0.9 indicates excellent intercoder reliability referring to previous content analysis (Garner, Davidson, & Williams, 2008; Han, 2018; Kracker & Pollio, 2003). The two coders negotiated each instance of coding difference until an agreement was reached, and finalized the coding result.

3.3.2 Subject, Task Type and Complexity of Topics

The coding results of the information problem dimension shows the topic features in terms of *Subject, Type, Complexity of Knowledge Dimension*, and *Complexity of Cognitive Dimension*.

Among the descriptions from the 343 replies, 321 respondents mentioned which subject they searched for across devices. By the second round of coding, subjects were classified based on the primary-level and secondary-level categories of the Curlie Directory (www.curlie.org). Curlie is a multilingual online directory of world wide web links, like Google Directory and DOMZ Directory, both of which had already been discontinued. The Curlie Directory contains a list of hierarchical taxonomies, including 16 primary-level categories (Arts, Business, Computers, Games, Home, Health, News, Recreation, Reference, Regional, Science, Shopping, Society, Sports, Kids & Teens Directory, and Curlie around the World) and a set of corresponding sub-categories.

Figure 3.1 presents the subject distribution of cross-device search topics, and shows that the most frequently-searched category is Arts, followed by Shopping, Reference, and Computers. As the primary category provides little specific information, we further analyzed the secondary-level categories of Arts, Shopping, Reference, and Computers. Cross-device searches on Arts include comics, literature, movies, music, television, video, and visual arts. Users attempted to find online or download resources about these categories. Shopping-related searches mainly relate to different aspects of living, such as clothing, food, home, and vehicles. One possible reason for the high occurrence of Shopping is that two shopping "festivals," 11.11 in China and Black Friday in the USA, are included in the survey period. With regard to Reference searches, 67.44% (29/43) are about education, including information on qualification examinations, explanation of terminologies, and professional articles. Searches on Computers can be categorized into two situations: to find a website and to solve a problem regarding network or software. For example, "i think last week i searched the same topic different devices. its wireless adapter," and "I had to search for what was going on with how pages were sticking and then just closing randomly."

The coding of *Type* resulted from respondents' own choices. The options provided were factual task (specific question and specific answer), interpretive task (specific question and general answer), and exploratory task (general question and general answer). Table 3.6 shows that nearly half of the cross-device searches reported in the survey are factual tasks, and interpretive and exploratory tasks account for almost equal proportions of the other half. Compared to interpretive and exploratory tasks, the information needs of a factual task with a specific answer should be less complex. Searching factual tasks across different devices is

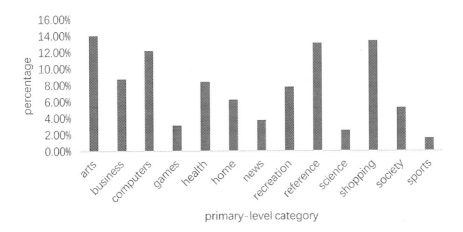

FIGURE 3.1 Search subjects of cross-device search topics

34 Cross-device Search Topics

TABLE 3.6 Task types of cross-device search topics

Task type	Frequency	Percentage (%)
Factual	159	46
Interpretive	89	26
Exploratory	95	28

likely to be driven less by complex information needs and more by other forces. Table 3.3 also shows that task types with specific questions, namely factual and interpretive tasks, predominate. This finding indicates that cross-device search is generated from the clear motivation of solving a problem.

Participants were asked to judge the complexity of the reported cross-device search experience simultaneously, and the results are shown in Table 3.7. For the knowledge dimension, half of the cross-device search topics are at the lowest level of complexity, which was searching for factual knowledge. This is consistent with the analysis of task type. For the cognitive dimension, cross-device search topics mainly occur at the middle stages of the cognitive process, which are "understand," "apply," and "analyze." With regard to the complexity of both the knowledge and cognitive processes, it was found that most cross-device search topics involve searching for factual knowledge at the "analyze" stage of cognition. We can conclude that the complexity of cross-device search topics depends more heavily on the user's cognitive state than on knowledge complexity.

3.3.3 Context of Topics

Besides the features of the topic itself, we also investigated features of the topic context. This is because the occurrence of cross-device search is closely related to search context. For example, changes in search location can drive users to change search devices. Device switching is also a necessary context for a cross-device search, which distinguishes it from a general web search. We examined the coding results of *Environment* and *Device Switch* to uncover context features.

During the coding of *Environment*, we determined whether there was a change of search location according to the relevant narrative in the cross-device search experience description. If more than one location was mentioned or an obvious expression of location shift occurred, we coded "changed place." For example, Respondent 206 stated: "*searched for a recipe of corn chowder at my work computer on google. then got home in the kitchen and turned around and looked for the recipe again….*" Conversely, if only one location was mentioned and there was no expression of location shift, we coded "unchanged place." For example, Respondent 272 stated: "*I was at home typing up some work on my home computer when one of my kids approached me with a school work problem… so I started looking it up on my computer. While it was loading I grabbed my tablet and looked up youtube so we could watch a video of the science behind this phenomena.*" In total, we coded 42 changed places and 64 unchanged places. Previous studies reported that location shift was a reason why users search on

TABLE 3.7 Task complexity of cross-device search topics

		Cognitive process dimension						
		Remember (%)	Understand (%)	Apply (%)	Analyze (%)	Evaluate (%)	Create (%)	Total (%)
Knowledge dimension	Factual knowledge	7	10	9	17	6	1	50
	Conceptual knowledge	2	7	7	5	1	2	24
	Procedural knowledge	1	3	8	4	2	2	20
	Metacognitive knowledge	1	1	1	2	2	0	6
	Total	11	20	25	28	11	4	100

36 Cross-device Search Topics

multiple devices. Our coding results show that there is no major difference between the number of cross-device search tasks with and without location changes.

As shown in Table 3.8, there are 12 directions of switching devices among the 342 replies (one outlier switched from a PS4 to a laptop). Devices used in cross-device searches were mainly smartphones, desktops, and laptops. For the pre-switch device, smartphones are undoubtedly in a dominant position. and desktops and laptops are used nearly equally. For the post-switch device, the gap between smartphones and desktops/laptops narrows. We found that users prefer smartphones as the initial device for cross-device searches. There are two frequent ways in which device switching occurs: smartphone to laptop and smartphone to desktop. This finding demonstrates a frequent device switch direction, which is mobile to desktop in a cross-device search. Users prefer the smartphone as the initial search device because of its portability, accessibility, and privacy. In the age of the 5G network, people are inseparable from their smartphones. Additionally, in many workplaces, employees are not allowed to use work computers to deal with private matters. Therefore, smartphones have become the first choice for searching.

3.3.4 Intent and Motivation of Topics

The *Goal* category involves the situation in which participants decided to perform a search. Analyzing this situation helps to understand the purpose of and motivation for conducting cross-device search tasks. Reasons for switching devices to resume a topic search were coded *Switching Reasons*, which reflects what motivates a cross-device search. Thus, we analyzed the intent and motivation of cross-device search topics through these two categories.

Among the replies, 114 descriptions reported the search situation, from which we conclude the following purposes: for buying, for eating, for learning, for traveling, for working, for fixing, and for helping. Users search for various information with the ultimate purpose of buying products, as stated by Respondent 207: "*I searched the nearest food store because I needed to go grocery shopping.*" Another person searched for a review of a product with the same objective of buying, as stated by Respondent 249: "*To know about the best review of online product i have used mobile app and the laptop browser to evaluate product.*" This finding implies that, to some extent, the search subject cannot reveal the goal of the search. Furthermore, the search subject and search goal represent different characteristics of information needs.

TABLE 3.8 Device switch of cross-device search topics

Post Pre	Smartphone (%)	Tablet/iPad (%)	Laptop (%)	Desktop (%)	Total (%)
Smartphone	—	6	30	25	60
Tablet/iPad	1	—	0	1	2
Laptop	18	1	—	1	20
Desktop	16	1	1	—	18
Total	35	8	30	27	100

For the eating purpose, searching was about recipes and restaurants, according to *"I searched for a recipe at home and decided to make it for my family"* by Respondent 277 and *"I was searching for a restaurant to take my family for dinner"* by Respondent 265. For the learning purpose, participants were in a situation where they engaged in an activity and wanted to know related information. Respondent 300 was listening to music and was suddenly interested in the group performing it (*"I was listening to some good music and I was interested in learning something more about that music group"*). For the traveling purpose, participants searched for hotels, flights, tourist attractions, etc. The working purpose involved searching in order to deal with problems at work or to find a job; for example, *"I was on a service call with a customer and needed to look up some information pertaining to the device I was there to repair"* (Respondent 231), and *"I needed some information for a job right away…"* (Respondent 274). For the fixing purpose, an example is the description from Respondent 267: *"I was in my car with my friend and we had got a sudden flat tire."* The helping purpose occurred among participants who were parents. They searched to help their children with school assignments; for example, Respondent 250 stated: *"I was searching a topic for my son for his school assignment…"*

The category of *Switching Reasons* was coded based on both the description of Q2 and options of Q10. In our previous cross-device search user experiment (Wu, Dong, & Tang, 2018), we identified several reasons why users perform cross-device searches, and these are the options in Q10:

(1) A planned cross-device search ("Planned"), where the user expects to use different devices before performing the search. This occurs when the user wants to double check or to search quickly. For example, Respondent 303 stated: *"I used my phone to double check a price on an airline site…"* and Respondent 336 stated: *"The reason I decided to use two different devices was because I had heard about controversy with a film and wanted to check it out quickly."*

(2) Unsatisfied information needs ("Unsatisfied"), where the user does not obtain the needed information on the anterior device. Respondent 230 stated: *"I searched it on laptop because I was not satisfied with search results of phone browser."*

(3) Helping memory ("Memory"), where the user searches on the posterior device in order to remember what he/she had seen on the anterior device. It is possible that a person searches for a topic and after a while forgets some of the details. Respondent 280 forgot some of the steps for installing Linux on a PC, which he had searched for on a PC, so he searched again on a phone. Respondent 339 searched for a movie on a laptop. When driving to the cinema, she forgot the movie time and searched for it on her smartphone.

(4) Forced to interrupt the search ("Forced"), where the search on the anterior device is suddenly interrupted, so the user has to resume the search on another device. Interruption varied according to replies, including other activities (Respondent 282: *"I had to stop and get my kids ready for bed"*), internet connection problems (Respondent 289: *"I ended up switching computers because the desktop I started on ended up losing wireless connection"*), running out of power (Respondent 155: "后来手机没电了" [after a while my phone was out of power]), etc.

(5) Complementing existing search results ("Complement"), where the user expects to acquire more information by searching on another device, even if he/she has found the needed information on the anterior device. This indicates that new needs arise during a cross-device search. When the user finds relevant results on the anterior device, he/she may want to compare or verify them by searching on the posterior device. According to Respondent 232: *"I compared the results to see the similarities and the differences in the selections."* Moreover, the user might wish to obtain more information, something he/she had not expected to search for initially, as Respondent 239 stated: *"Then when I got to the store I realized I didn't know where they were so I searched for them on my phone to get the aisle number that they were on."*

Figure 3.2 shows the frequency of these five reasons. The predominant reason for the cross-device search is unsatisfied information needs, followed by a wish to complement existing search results, a planned cross-device search, being forced to interrupt the search, and helping memory.

In addition to these five reasons, we coded three more reasons from the "Others" option, according to the description of Q2:

(6) Device advantage ("Advantage"), where the user decides to search on another device because of either the limitations of the anterior device or the advantages of the posterior device. According to the descriptions for this reason, participants expressed frequent complaints about smartphones, such as inconvenient for typing, the inability to open many tabs, uncomfortable scrolling, small screen, and so on. Meanwhile, the portability of smartphones and tablets was mentioned.
(7) User preference ("Preference"), where the user changes the search device because he/she prefers not to use one device for a long time. Only one participant (Respondent 95) claimed her device switch resulted from the uncomfortable feeling of using one device for a long time.

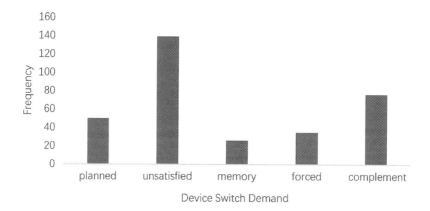

FIGURE 3.2 Device switch demand for cross-device search topics

(8) Access to device ("Access"), where the user loses access to the anterior device, so he/she has to change the search device. As stated by Respondent 263: "I performed the search using my laptop computer but i also used my apple iphone as well when i was away from the computer…"

3.3.5 Process of Topic Search

The coding results of the information-seeking process dimension present users' behavioral features during the process of cross-device search topics, which comprises the categories *Pre-switch Device*, *Post-switch Device*, *Search System*, *Issued Query*, *Visited Page*, and *Outcome*. Additionally, we include the analysis of the category *Switching Interval* which is part of the topic search.

The results for the *Pre-switch Device* and *Post-switch Device* were used to code the *Device Switch* in the Episodes dimension; the analysis can be seen in Section 3.3.3. Query and result pages are inevitable attributes of search activities. Although only 17 description texts included the specific queries that the user issued, Table 3.9 reveals the number of queries issued before and after the device switch. In addition, Table 3.10 presents the number of pages visited before and after the device switch. As shown, most users tend to submit multiple queries and visit multiple pages during a cross-device search. The number of queries issued and pages visited almost remains the same between the pre-switch and post-switch. Although the number may not be as precise as data collected by transaction logs, this result still implies a small number of interactions during the cross-device search.

The category *Outcome* gathers content about the users' discussion at the end of a cross-device search. The second-round coding of *Outcome* includes content related to three aspects: comments on search results; evaluation of user experience; and lessons learned from the search described.

Among the comments on search results, participants stated whether they had found the information they wanted, such as Respondent 217 stating: "*finally i got my need*." On the other hand, participants reported the comparison of results between two devices. Obtaining different results when searching

TABLE 3.9 Queries issued in cross-device search topics

Post-switch \\ *Pre-switch*	1–2 (%)	3–4 (%)	5–6 (%)	More than 6 (%)	Total (%)
1–2	52	11	1	0	64
3–4	11	11	3	1	26
5–6	1	1	1	1	4
More than 6	0	1	0	3	5
Total	64	25	6	5	100

40 Cross-device Search Topics

TABLE 3.10 Visited page of cross-device search topics

Pre-switch / Post-switch	1–5 (%)	6–10 (%)	11–15 (%)	More than 15 (%)	Total (%)
1–5	55	15	1	1	72
6–10	10	8	2	0	21
11–15	1	1	1	0	4
More than 15	0	1	0	2	4
Total	66	25	5	4	100

for the same task across different devices can cause confusion for users, which should be resolved in order to improve user experience. According to Respondent 259: "*I got the same results on each device,*" and Respondent 350: "*I got two different weather reports. I do not know which one I should believe.*" Moreover, participants cared a great deal about advertisements and the thoroughness of the results, according to Respondent 3: "百度广告不少,但是还是能找到答案 (There were many ads on Baidu, but I still found the answer)" and Respondent 260: "*I found the page to have more details displayed, when accessed through the tablet.*"

Terms that frequently occurred when users evaluated their experience are "satisfied," "success," "quick," and "easy." Satisfaction and the success of the search indicate how completely information needs are fulfilled, which estimates the quality of search results. Quick and easy searching indicates how efficient the search process is, which evaluates the quality of the search process. It is concluded that the quality of the user experience is associated with both the search process and search results.

Some respondents discussed what they had learned. For example, Respondent 265 stated: "*If I want to view more information or in any detail, I will use my laptop as the results are more detailed and specific.*" Respondent 267 stated: "*It was helpful to have the larger screen to see things more clearly.*"

Switching Interval was further coded as "within an hour" and "over an hour," with 250 participants claiming they switched devices within an hour and the remaining 93 claiming it was over an hour. For within an hour, the average interval is 18.51 minutes (standard deviation = 11.36). For over an hour, excluding four replies for over 24 hours, the average interval is 2.65 hours (standard deviation = 2.30). Therefore, we examined the distribution of the switching interval in terms of within an hour and over an hour, in units of 20 minutes and 3 hours, respectively. From Figure 3.3, we can see that users are likely to resume their search on another device either within 40 minutes or in 1 to 3 hours. This provides a reference to identify sessions of cross-device search from transaction logs.

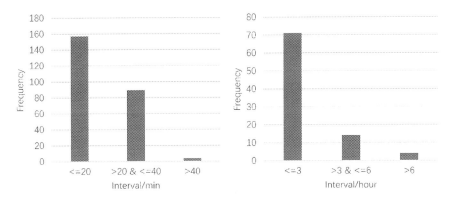

FIGURE 3.3 Switching intervals of cross-device search topics (left: distribution within an hour; right: distribution over an hour)

3.4 Cross-device Search Topic Collection Development

3.4.1 Correlation among Topic and Context Features

This sections describes the correlation tests among the features of cross-device search topics and context, namely *Subject, Type, Complexity of Knowledge Dimension, Complexity of Cognitive Dimension, Environment, Device Switch,* and *Switching Reasons*. These correlations can support the cross-device search topic collection design. As these variables are either nominal or ordinal, we used crosstab analysis to test statistical significance. The results can be seen in Tables 3.8–3.10.

As shown in Table 3.11, there is a significant correlation between subject and complexity, regardless of dimension. In-depth analysis of the co-occurrence indicates that the subjects occurring most frequently in complexity of factual knowledge are Health and Reference. For complexity of conceptual knowledge, the top subject is Arts. Computers occurs the most in the complexity of procedural knowledge. As

TABLE 3.11 Contingency coefficients among features of topic

Variable 1	Variable 2	Contingency coefficient (sig. * < 0.05)
Subject	Type	0.309 (0.087)
Subject	Complexity of Knowledge Dimension	0.389 (0.007*)
Subject	Complexity of Cognitive Dimension	0.470 (0.006*)
Type	Complexity of Knowledge Dimension	0.410 (0.000*)
Type	Complexity of Cognitive Dimension	0.217 (0.077)

42 Cross-device Search Topics

for the complexity of metacognitive knowledge, the occurrence of different subjects is low and similar, the top one being Arts.

From the point of view of the cognitive dimension, Arts-related searches occur the most in the complexity of "remember." Reference is likely associated with the complexity of "understand." Shopping is the most frequent subject in the complexity of "apply." Business co-occurs the most with the complexity of "analyze." For the complexity of "evaluate," Recreation is the prominent subject, while Home is the top subject in the complexity of "create." There is a significant correlation between task type and the complexity of knowledge dimension. It can be expected that the factual task occurs the most in the complexity of factual knowledge. Interpretive tasks are the highest in the complexity of conceptual knowledge. Exploratory tasks are prominent in the complexity of metacognitive knowledge.

Table 3.12 shows a significant correlation only between *Device Switch* and *Switching Reasons*. The top device switches for each switching demand are: desktop–smartphone and a planned cross-device search, smartphone–laptop and unsatisfied information needs, laptop–smartphone and helping memory, laptop–smartphone and forced to interrupt the search, smartphone–laptop/desktop and complementing existing search results, smartphone–laptop and device advantage, laptop–desktop and user preference, and desktop–smartphone and access to device.

As shown in Table 3.13, search subjects are significantly correlated with *Environment* and *Device Switch*. Moreover, *Switching Reasons* shows a significant correlation with *Complexity of Cognitive Dimension*. The top subjects that co-occurred with changed place include Home, Recreation, Reference, and Shopping. Meanwhile, Arts, Computers, Shopping, and Society were the top four subjects with an unchanged place. With both changed place and unchanged place, cross-device search topics about Shopping occurred frequently. In fact, whether or not there is a location shift depends on whether the shopping activity is online or offline. Home is associated with a changed place because many tasks involved searching for recipes, and users tend to come to the kitchen from other rooms. Recreation includes Travel, and users tend to make plans at home and search for details after leaving. Reference searches are regularly performed at work and at home. Arts searches frequently focus on movies and e-books, and users seek entertainment in a stable and comfortable setting. Computers searches specifically concern fixing computer problems. Users tend to search while manipulating, so the search place is fixed. Society searches are regularly about factual information, so they can be quickly completed in a single location.

TABLE 3.12 Contingency coefficient among features of topic context

Variable 1	Variable 2	Contingency coefficient (sig. * < 0.05)
Environment	Device Switch	0.317 (0.373)
Environment	Switching Reasons	0.238 (0.382)
Device Switch	Switching Reasons	0.680 (0.000*)

TABLE 3.13 Contingency coefficients between topic and context

Contingency coefficient (sig. ★ < 0.05)	Environment	Device Switch	Switching Reasons
Subject	0.499 (0.001★)	0.610 (0.006★)	0.484 (0.138)
Type	0.100 (0.584)	0.286 (0.331)	0.202 (0.404)
Complexity of Knowledge Dimension	0.190 (0.266)	0.265 (0.896)	0.286 (0.082)
Complexity of Cognitive Dimension	0.168 (0.689)	0.389 (0.430)	0.414 (0.000★)

For frequently-occurring device switches, the corresponding top search subjects are smartphone–laptop and Business, smartphone–desktop and Shopping, laptop–smartphone and Arts, desktop–smartphone and Arts/Shopping, and smartphone–tablet and Reference. Additionally, the most frequent complexities occurring for each switching demand are: "understand" and a planned cross-device search, "analyze" and unsatisfied information needs, "remember" and helping memory, "apply" and forced to interrupt the search, "analyze" and complement existing search results, and "apply" and device advantage. The complexity co-occurrence of user preference and access to device is very low, and this is difficult to explain.

3.4.2 Developing Topic Collection Based on Correlations

Search tasks are essential components of information search user studies. Among many studies, researchers recruit participants to conduct one or more search tasks and collect behavioral data by logs, questionnaires, interviews, etc. Some utilize search tasks in previous studies as reference, and some design new tasks on their own. Although what the tasks describe and require can be seen, there are few tutorials about how to design appropriate search tasks in detail. Therefore, it is important to fill the lack of guidance about generating search tasks. Search activities depend heavily on context. For instance, previous comparative studies have found different search patterns on desktop, mobile, and tablet devices (Song, Ma, Wang, & Wang, 2013). Moreover, an eye-tracking analysis revealed different levels of eye movement and search performance between desktop and mobile searches (Kim, Thomas, Sankaranarayana, Gedeon, & Yoon, 2015). Therefore, it is necessary to account for context.

As for cross-device search topics/tasks, the device transition is an explicit factor of constructing context, while intent and motivation are implicit factors. In our experience, it is difficult to provoke an authentic information need by conducting user experiments in labs. Participants in a lab experiment are searching in order to complete the assignment, rather than to satisfy an information need as they would

44 Cross-device Search Topics

in a real situation. Participants who are given only the topic itself might be confused about the purpose during the process of searching the assigned task. It is suggested that designing for cross-device search tasks should explain the intent and motivation of the search in order to make the context clear to participants.

Referring to test collections of information retrieval evaluation frameworks such as TREC, CLEF, NTCIR etc., we described topics in the form of XML. The structure of topic description is shown in Figure 3.4.

The features of the topic itself were firstly considered into the topic design, which refer to the categories of *Subject, Type, Complexity of Knowledge Dimension* and *Complexity of Cognitive Dimension*. Tag <number> refers to serial numbers of each topic in the collection. Father tag <subject> maps category *Subject*, consisting of three son tags <primary>, <sub> and <title>. The values of <primary> and <sub> correspond to the primary-level and secondary-level categories of the Curlie Directory. Tag <title> is a term we concluded from the user's search

```
<topic >
<number>2</number>
<subject>
    <primary>games</primary>
    <sub>computer games</sub>
    <title>"Dead Island "Strategy Guide</title>
</subject>
<type>factual</type>
<complexity>
    <knowledge>conceptual</knowledge >
    <cognitive>understand</cognitive>
    <outcome>list(set)</outcome>
    <mental activities>identify, compile</mental activities>
</complexity>
<narrative>

"Dead Island" is your favorite computer game, but somehow you are
stuck on one mission named "game sky". In order to finish this mission,
you search the strategy of it on your laptop immediately. And then you
turn on the game and search it again on your smartphone.
</narrative>
<search system>Baidu</search system>
<goal> for learning</goal>
<device switch>laptop to smartphone</device switch>
<switching reasons> planned cross-device search</switching reasons>
</topic>
```

FIGURE 3.4 Topic structure and example

experience description. Tag <type> maps category *Type*, describing the search task type. Values of <type> include factual, interpretive and exploratory. Father tag <complexity> maps the categories *Complexity of Knowledge Dimension* and *Complexity of Cognitive Dimension;* thus, there are two son tags, <knowledge> and <cognitive>. Values of <knowledge> are factual knowledge, conceptual knowledge, procedural knowledge, and metacognitive knowledge.

Meanwhile, values of <cognitive> are remember, understand, apply, analyze, evaluate, and create. This generates an issue that facing given values of tag <cognitive>, it is possible for users to be confused about what exactly the task requires by those complexities. We were inspired by the task designing method proposed by Kelly, Arguello, Edwards, & Wu (2015), which also adopts the cognitive process dimension of Krathwohl's Taxonomy (Krathwohl, 2002) to construct search tasks. They distinguished different complexities of cognition from two dimensions of outcome and mental activity, which were introduced in our topic description structure. Values of tags <outcome> and <mental activities>, corresponding to each cognitive complexity, are shown in Table 3.14.

Remember tasks require the searcher to identify or recognize a fact as it occurs in an information source. Understand tasks require the searcher to provide an exhaustive list of items. Similar to remember tasks, this type of task primarily requires the searcher to identify a list or factors in an information source and possibly compile the list from multiple sources if a single list cannot be found. Apply tasks require searchers to identify and compile steps of solving a problem and describe the manipulation of each step. Analyze tasks require the searcher to find and compile a list of items and to understand and describe their differences. Evaluate tasks require the searcher to find and compile a list of items, understand their differences, and make a recommendation. The outcome for Create tasks is a plan, which requires the searcher to perform the same sets of actions for the Evaluate tasks, except instead of a justification the searcher needs to generate something.

Features of topic context, intent, and motivation were also considered in the topic design. Tags of <search system>, <device switch>, <goal> and <switching reasons> correspond to the coded categories. Values of <search system> could be

TABLE 3.14 <outcome> and <mental activities> corresponding to <cognitive>

Cognitive complexity	Outcome	Mental activities
Remember	Fact	Identify
Understand	List(set)	Identify, compile
Apply	List(step), description	Identify, compile, describe
Analyze	List (prioritized), description	Identify, compile, describe
Evaluate	Recommendation	Identify, compile, describe, compare, decide, justify
Create	Plan	Identify, compile, describe, compare, decide, make

46 Cross-device Search Topics

a given search engine or "unclear," depending on whether the survey responses offered the information. Values of <device switch> are comprised of 12 directions of switching device coded in the survey, which are smartphone to tablet/iPad, smartphone to laptop, smartphone to desktop, tablet/iPad to smartphone, tablet/iPad to laptop, tablet/iPad to desktop, laptop to smartphone, laptop to tablet/iPad, laptop to desktop, desktop to smartphone, desktop to tablet/iPad and desktop to laptop. Values of <goal> are seven different coded goals, including for buying, for eating, for learning, for traveling, for working, for fixing, and for helping. Values of <switching reasons> are eight coded reasons: a planned cross-device search, unsatisfied information needs, helping memory, forced to interrupt the search, complementing existing search results, device advantage, user preference, and access to device. In addition to tags about features of topic itself, context, intent and motivation, <narrative> refers to a text describing the task according to those feature tags.

We created the topic collection (see Appendix) based on topics extracted from 343 users' real-situation cross-device searches, which were collected by the crowdsourcing survey. Values of each tag were determined based on the descriptions and survey responses of 343 users. Figure 3.4 shows a topic example, which requires the searcher to find information about a computer game called "Dead Island." The purpose is to learn the strategy of passing a mission called "game sky," which is a specific question with specific answer. Tag <switching reasons> implies the searcher intends to use different search devices before beginning to search, which is from laptop to smartphone. The outcome requires the searcher to compile information from multiple sources and list a set of game strategies.

Currently, although our topic collection consists of 343 topics extracted from the survey, the collection can be extended based on correlations between different features. Statistical tests show that *Subject* has a significant correlation with *Complexity of Knowledge Dimension, Complexity of Cognitive Dimension, Environment*, and *Device Switch. Type* has a significant correlation with *Complexity of Knowledge Dimension. Switching Reasons* has a significant correlation with *Device Switch* and *Complexity of Cognitive Dimension*. According to the identified co-occurrences, different subjects should be taken into account when researchers design search tasks, varying in terms of complexity, environment, and device switches. For example, Health and Reference are the subjects most likely to correspond with the complexity of factual knowledge, so the factual knowledge search task should concern Health or Reference. Similarly, different task types should be designed for the corresponding complexity of the knowledge dimension. The best combinations are factual tasks and the complexity of factual knowledge, interpretive tasks and the complexity of conceptual knowledge, and exploratory tasks and the complexity of metacognitive knowledge. Correlations between *Switching Reasons* and *Device Switch/Complexity of Cognitive Dimension* indicate that, given a device switch direction or the level of task complexity of the cognition dimension, it is reasonable to provide a corresponding context for switching.

Cross-device Search Topics **47**

3.5 Summary

In information retrieval evaluation campaigns like TREC, topics are used to describe a search task represented by task type and subject. Similarly, the topic in this chapter is a broad term similar to the concept of task. This chapter explores cross-device search behavior through the characteristics of cross-device search topics, and collects descriptions of real-situation cross-device search experiences by a global crowdsourcing survey.

A total of 343 valid responses were used for the content analysis, and the coding scheme was grounded in the Multiple Information Seeking Episodes (MISE) model, which was proposed to explain successive multiple-episode searching. Characteristics of cross-device search topics were uncovered by coded categories of *Subject, Type, Complexity of Knowledge Dimension, Complexity of Cognitive Dimension, Environment, Device Switch*, and *Switching Reasons*. The results show the most frequently-searched topics are Arts, Shopping, Reference, and Computers. Task types focus on factual tasks, indicating a clear information need. Task complexity depends heavily on the user's cognition.

Eight reasons for switching device are identified in order to understand device switch demand (see Table 3.15). Finally, statistical tests show significant correlations among the characteristics. *Subject* has a significant correlation with *Complexity*

TABLE 3.15 Summary of eight switching reasons

Switching reasons	*Note*
A planned cross-device search ("Planned")	The user expects to use different devices before performing the search.
Unsatisfied information needs ("Unsatisfied")	The user does not obtain the information needed on the anterior device.
Helping memory ("Memory")	The user searches to the posterior device in order to remember what he/she had seen on the anterior device.
Forced to interrupt the search ("Forced")	The search on the anterior device is suddenly interrupted, so the user has to resume the search on another device.
Complementing existing search results ("Complement")	The user expects to acquire more information by searching on another device, even if he/she has found the information needed on the anterior device.
Device advantage ("Advantage")	The user decides to search to another device because of either the limitations of the anterior device or the advantages of the posterior device.
User preference ("Preference")	The user changes the search device because he/she prefers not to use one device for a long time.
Access to device ("Access")	The user loses access to the anterior device, so he/she has to change the search device.

48 Cross-device Search Topics

of Knowledge Dimension, Complexity of Cognitive Dimension, Environment, and *Device Switch. Type* has a significant correlation with *Complexity of Knowledge Dimension. Switching Reasons* has a significant correlation with *Device Switch* and *Complexity of Cognitive Dimension.* The cross-device search topic collection is developed based on these correlations.

Reference

Beitzel, S. M., Jensen, E. C., Chowdhury, A., Grossman, D., & Frieder, A. (2004, July). Hourly analysis of a very large topically categorized web query log. In *The 27th Annual International ACM SIGIR Conference on Research and Development in Information* Retrieval, UK (pp. 321–328). doi:10.1145/1008992.1009048

Byström, K., & Järvelin, K. (1995). Task complexity affects information seeking and use. *Information Processing & Management, 31,* 191–213. doi:10.1016/0306-4573(95)80035-R

Campbell, D. J. (1988). Task complexity: A review and analysis. *Academy of Management Review, 13*(1), 40–52. doi:10.5465/amr.1988.4306775

Chau, M., Fang, X., & Sheng, O. (2005). Analysis of the query logs of a web site search engine. *Journal of the Association for Information Science & Technology, 56*(13), 1363–1376. doi:10.1002/asi.20210

Estellés-Arolas, E., & González-Ladrón-De-Guevara, F. (2012). Towards an integrated crowdsourcing definition. *Journal of Information Science, 38*(2), 189–200. doi:10.1177/0165551512437638

Garner, J., Davidson, K., & Williams, V. K. (2008). Identifying serials trends through twenty years of NASIG conference proceedings: A content analysis. *Serials Review, 34*(2), 88–103. doi:10.1016/j.serrev.2007.12.007

Gwizdka, J., & Spence, I. (2006). What can searching behavior tell us about the difficulty of information tasks? A study of web navigation. *Proceedings of the American Society for Information Science and Technology, 43*(1), 1–22. doi:10.1002/meet.14504301167

Han, H. (2018). Children's help-seeking behaviors and effects of domain knowledge in using Google and Kids.gov: Query formulation and results evaluation stages. *Library & Information Science Research, 40*(3–4), 208–218. doi:10.1016/j.lisr.2018.09.003

Hienert, D., Mitsui, M., Mayr, P., Shah, C., & Belkin, N. J. (2018). The role of the task topic in web search of different task types. In *Proceedings of the 2018 Conference on Human Information Interaction & Retrieval.* (pp. 72–81). doi:10.1145/3176349.3176382

Howe, J. (2006). The rise of crowdsourcing. *Wired Magazine, 14,* 1–5.

Jansen, B. J., Liu, Z., Weaver, C., Campbell, G., & Gregg, M. (2011). Real time search on the web: Queries, topics, and economic value. *Information Processing and Management, 47*(4), 491–506. doi:10.1016/j.ipm.2011.01.007

Kellar, M., Watters, C., & Shepherd, M. (2007). A field study characterizing web-based information-seeking tasks. *Journal of the Association for Information Science & Technology, 58*(7), 999–1018. doi:10.1002/asi.20590

Kelly, D., Arguello, J., Edwards, A., & Wu, W. (2015). Development and evaluation of search tasks for IIR experiments using a cognitive complexity framework. In *Proceedings of the 2015 International Conference on The Theory of Information Retrieval (ICTIR '15)* (pp. 101–110). doi:10.1145/2808194.2809465

Kim, J. (2006, April). Task difficulty as a predictor and indicator of Web searching interaction. In *Extended Abstracts on Human Factors in Computing Systems,* Canada (pp. 959–964). doi:10.1145/1125451.1125636

Kim, J., Thomas, P., Sankaranarayana, R., Gedeon, T., & Yoon, H.-J. (2015). Eye-tracking analysis of user behavior and performance in web search on large and small screens. *Journal of the Association for Information Science and Technology, 66*, 526–544. doi:10.1002/asi.23187

Kittur, A., Chi, Ed H., & Suh, B. (2008, April). Crowdsourcing user studies with mechanical turk. In *The SIGCHI Conference on Human Factors in Computing Systems*, Italy (pp. 453–456). doi:10.1145/1357054.1357127

Kracker, J., & Pollio, H. R. (2003). The experience of libraries across time: Thematic analysis of undergraduate recollections of library experiences. *Journal of the Association for Information Science and Technology, 54*(12), 1104–1116. doi:10.1002/asi.10309

Krathwohl, D. R. (2002). A revision of Bloom's taxonomy: An overview. *Theory Into Practice, 41*(4), 212–218. doi:10.1207/s15430421tip4104_2

Li, L., Deng, H., He, Y., Dong, A., Chang, Y., & Zha, H. (2016). Behavior driven topic transition for search task identification. In *International Conference on World Wide Web* (pp. 555–565). doi:10.1145/2872427.2883047

Li, Y., & Belkin, N. J. (2008). A faceted approach to conceptualizing tasks in information seeking. *Information Processing and Management, 44*(6), 1822–1837. doi:10.1016/j.ipm.2008.07.005

Li, Y., & Belkin, N. J. (2010). An exploration of the relationships between work task and interactive information search behavior. *Journal of the American Society for Information Science and Technology, 61*(9), 1771–1789. doi:10.1002/asi.21359

Li, Y., Chen, Y., Liu, J., Cheng, Y., Wang, X., Chen, P., & Wang, Q. (2011). Measuring task complexity in information search from user's perspective. *Proceedings of the American Society for Information Science & Technology, 48*(1), 1–8. doi:10.1002/meet.2011.14504801092

Liang, S., & Leng, Y. (2020). Search topic analysis of ACM digital library. In *Proceedings of the ACM/IEEE Joint Conference on Digital Libraries in 2020 (JCDL '20)* (pp. 487–488). doi:10.1145/3383583.3398576

Lin, S. J., & Belkin, N. J. (2005). Validation of a model of information seeking over multiple search sessions. *Journal of the American Society for Information Science and Technology, 56*(4), 393–415. doi:10.1002/asi.20127

Liu, J., Gwizdka, J., Liu, C., & Belkin, N. J. (2010). Predicting task difficulty for different task types. *Proceedings of the American Society for Information Science and Technology, 47*(1), 1–10. doi:10.1002/meet.14504701173

Liu, J., Liu, C., & Belkin, N. (2013). Examining the effects of task topic familiarity on searchers' behaviors in different task types. *Proceedings of the American Society for Information Science and Technology, 50*(1), 1–10. doi:10.1002/meet.14505001033

Montañez, G. D., White, R. W., & Huang, X. (2014, November). Cross-device search. In *ACM International Conference on Conference on Information & Knowledge Management*, China (pp. 1669–1678). doi:10.1145/2661829.2661910

Mosenthal, P. B. (1998). Defining prose task characteristics for use in computer-adaptive testing and instruction. *American Educational Research Journal, 35*(2), 269–307. doi:10.3102/00028312035002269

Ozmutlu, S. (2006). Automatic new topic identification using multiple linear regression. *Information Processing & Management, 42*(4), 934–950. doi:10.1016/j.ipm.2005.10.002

Scott, W. A. (1955). Reliability of content analysis: The case of nominal scale coding. *Public Opinion Quarterly, 19*(3), 321–325. doi:10.1086/266577

Song, Y., Ma, H., Wang, H., & Wang, K. (2013). Exploring and exploiting user search behavior on mobile and tablet devices to improve search relevance. In *Proceedings of the 22nd International Conference on World Wide Web (WWW '13)* (pp. 1201–1212). doi:10.1145/2488388.2488493

50 Cross-device Search Topics

Taylor, R. S. (1962). The process of asking questions. *American Documentation, 14*(4), 391–396. doi:10.1002/asi.5090130405

Vakkari, P., & Kuokkanen, M. (1997). Theoretical growth in information science: Applications of the theory of science to a theory of information seeking. *Journal of Documentation, 53*(5), 497–519. doi:10.1108/EUM0000000007210

Wang, Y., Huang, X., & White, R. W. (2013, February). Characterizing and supporting cross-device search tasks. In *ACM International Conference on Web Search & Data Mining*, Italy (pp. 707–716). doi:10.1145/2433396.2433484

Wildemuth. B. M. (2017). *Applications of social research methods to questions in information and library science* (2nd edition, p. 311). California: Libraries Unlimited

Wildemuth, B. M., Kelly, D., Boettcher, E., Moore, E., & Dimitrova, G. (2018). Examining the impact of domain and cognitive complexity on query formulation and reformulation. *Information Processing & Management, 54*(3), 433–450. doi:10.1016/j.ipm.2018.01.009

Wu, D., Dong, J., & Tang, Y. (2018, July). Modeling and analyzing information preparation behaviors in cross-device search. In *International Conference on Cross-cultural Design*, Las Vegas (pp. 232–249).

Wu, D., Liang, S., & Bi, R. (2018). Characterizing queries in cross-device OPAC search: A large-scale log study. *Library Hi Tech, 36*(3), 482–497. doi:10.1108/LHT-06-2017-0130

4

CROSS-DEVICE SEARCH SUPPORT TECHNIQUES AND SYSTEMS

4.1 Introduction of Existing Cross-device Search Systems

4.1.1 Cross-device Support System in Industry

The cross-device search system is used to support the user's cross-device interaction needs and assist users in completing cross-device tasks in different cross-device interaction scenarios. Cross-device interaction has become an important supporting function for smart device manufacturers to build product ecological chains in the industrial field. For example, Windows joined Cortana's cross-device usage settings from Windows 10; Google Analytics began to support cross-screen and cross-device visitor tracking; Apple has supported AirDrop since iOS 7; and Huawei has built in a multi-screen collaboration feature since EMUI 10.

To be more specific, AirDrop emerged in 2013 when Apple announced that iOS 7 devices could use AirDrop for shared transmissions at the Worldwide Developers Conference. It is a unique feature of Apple's iOS, iPad OS, and MacOS systems to share files between multiple devices, allowing users to easily transfer files between devices (like wireless network transfers) through AirDrop. Users only need to confirm that two devices have Bluetooth and Wi-Fi abilities, open AirDrop, select the pictures or files which need to be transferred, then select the target device for document transfer, and file transfer can be achieved in a short time (as shown in Figure 4.1). If users under the same Apple ID choose to "accept AirDrop", all devices that launch this Apple ID can receive content through the same app used to send content. For example, photos will appear in the Photos app on both iPhone and Mac, and a site opened in Safari will also update on all devices. The app link opens in the App Store even if one uses multiple devices, so that one can download or purchase this app.

DOI: 10.4324/9780429201677-4

FIGURE 4.1 Interface of AirDrop on Mac. https://www.idownloadblog.com/2020/01/07/how-to-use-airdrop-iphone-ipad-mac/

Nowadays, Apple can support more than 12 cross-device usages, including AirDrop, clipboard, call, auto-unlock, quick-draw continuous interoperability, camera interoperability, mark interoperability, etc. These functions cover a variety of cross-device interaction scenarios for users on mobile phones, tablets, and computers, which can meet a variety of cross-device needs, including retrieval, file transfer, web browsing, and work relay.

Similarly, when Huawei's system was updated to EMUI 10, it also supported multi-screen collaboration functions between multiple devices. However, Huawei's cross-device interaction scenarios are focused on the context of work scene development, due to the fact that working on a mobile phone is not always comfortable, especially when creating a presentation or modifying a report. Additionally, a phone lacks the resources of a laptop, and transferring data from one to the other can prove to be quite a hassle.

Huawei's multi-screen collaboration feature can transfer images, documents, or files between them with a simple drag and drop. This kind of multi-screen collaboration allows users to connect the smartphone to Matebook quickly and easily. The mobile's screen will be projected on the laptop in real time and users can control both devices at once using a keyboard and a mouse.

4.1.2 Cross-device Support Systems in Academia

In addition to the field of practical application, scholars have also explored cross-device interaction and retrieval systems in academic research, and developed cross-device retrieval systems to support their studies.

In 2005, Potter and Nieh (2005) presented Webpod at the International World Wide Web Conference. Webpod is a portable system that enables users to use the same persistent, personalized web-browsing session on any Internet-enabled device through its USB storage device. It can share a user's browsing session, including open windows, web history, and bookmarks, between PCs.

To analyze users' cross-device web search behavioral patterns and compare them to the patterns in desktop-to-desktop web search, Han, Yue, and He (2015) presented CrossSearch, a web search system for supporting cross-device and cross-session exploratory web searches. This system returns search results from Google mobile or general Google searches. It can log various mouse touch interactions, including hold, tap, double-tap, drag up/down/left/right, and pinch in/out.

4.2 Cross-device Search Support Techniques

4.2.1 Cross-device Tracking Techniques

Identifying the same user across devices is the basis for a system to assist users with cross-device search tasks. Only by completing user recognition on different devices can the retrieval behavior, search results, browsing preferences, and other contents be synchronized before and after device conversion, in order to provide users with a good cross-device interaction experience. Traditionally, in the context of single-device use, most website analysis tools determine visitors by cookies. A cookie is a text file stored in a visitor's browser that records the visitor's identity. The cookie used to define the visitor has a unique string of numbers, which is the visitor ID. This visitor ID returns to the server of the site analysis tool with other metrics each time the visitor visits the site or browses the pages.

However, in cross-screen tracking, this unique identity no longer comes from the visitor ID in the cookies. Instead, it depends on the unique identity of the visitor on the site. This unique identity usually comes from the visitor's landing account which includes username and password login systems, allowing users to log in to their accounts from different devices through personal credentials (Brookman, Rouge, Alva, & Yeung, 2017). When a visitor completes a sign on a website, their account is used as the visitor's unique identity ID. Also, the server will give the visitor the identity of a test when this visitor logs onto the site on another device. This allows the website to identify the visitor from the server side and calculate a user's browse behavior across devices, thereby achieving visitor tracking across devices.

However, another question arises. When a user does not complete the login operation, how can the user's cross-device operations be identified? Some research has mentioned probabilistic cross-device tracking, which relies on a variety of information from multiple devices (e.g. cookies, IP addresses, hardware identifiers, and device fingerprints), and statistical models to infer whether those devices are used by the same person or group of people (Neufeld, 2017; Nikiforakis et al., 2013; Zimmeck, Li, Kim, Bellovin, & Jebara, 2017).

4.2.2 Cross-device Search Support Methods Based on Context

In the context of cross-device search, device switching results in some obstacles, including loss of retrieval history, retrieval process, memory difficulty of retrieval results, etc. These obstacles make users want to be able to restore their previous task completion progress and problem states. The simplest way to solve this problem is to store the users' retrieval and browsing history, allowing users to quickly revisit the information they collected after they switched devices. There are two kinds of methods to assist users' page re-visitation experiences through the way mentioned above: Session Heights and Auto Web.

Session Heights was mainly implemented in JAVA 2 and generates graphics in a Scalable Vector Graphics (SVG) format through the Apache Batik SVG Toolkit. Users drag the Address icon and drop it anywhere in the workspace to add a URL. In this way, it helps users skim through the content they visited. However, because each page takes up a lot of space, this approach is not always efficient enough. Auto Web can automatically classify web pages into different groups based on content. Thus, users can quickly revisit an opened web page by narrowing down search scope into a group of pages that share the same topic.

People also frequently adopt note-taking, bookmarking functions for task resumption in the context of cross-device searching. Based on the requirements on the context of information re-visitation behaviors, some solutions have been proposed. SearchPad is a Yahoo! Application that was launched in 2009 and is present in Donato et al.'s study (Donato, Bonchi, Chi, & Maarek, 2010). It is a toolkit that automatically identifies research missions and presents a search workspace comprising previous queries and results related to the mission. SearchPad uses measures of topic coherence between pairs of consecutive queries and user engagement to identify such research missions. Specifically, SearchPad does not require users to use a dedicated plug-in, toolbar, or separate application, but is built in within the main search service of Yahoo!. Users will be required to sign-in only when saving a pad. This feature is helpful in reducing the adoption barrier for users.

Similarly, SearchBar is a toolkit designed by Morris et al. (2008), which can proactively and persistently store query histories, browsing histories, and users' notes and ratings. SearchBar supports multi-session investigations by integrated search and browsing history within the context of a web browser. It can monitor all navigation events, recognize URLs corresponding to common search engines, and track a user's browsing history after a search.

Chang and Li (2011) developed Deepshot, a tool that can be used to support a range of everyday tasks migrating across devices by taking pictures of a website from a desktop computer using a phone camera. Andolina, Klouche, Ruotsalo, Floréen, and Jacucci (2018) developed a multi-device collaborative search tool, QueryTogether, which can help users share queries to public screens or send them to specific users, and can realize easy to touch interaction. Gomes and Hoeber

Search Support Techniques and Systems **55**

(2021) designed a search interface of an academic digital library that supports cross-session and cross-device search, and uses visual methods to browse and select past search topics. The system can also help users use the faceted navigation function to investigate previously saved documents.

4.2.3 Cross-device Search-Related Patents

Cross-device search patents can reflect the cutting-edge aspect and current situation of cross-device search-related technology development. Table 4.1 summarizes some of the relevant patent information. Current cross-device search patents consist of cross-device storage of resources, information fusion in the context of cross-devices, fast and efficient cross-device user identification, and so on.

TABLE 4.1 Some patents of cross-device search

Patent	Patent number	Advantages
Cross-device link aggregation local forwarding system utilizing method; involves utilizing VP port to perform secondary search in VP mapping table to find corresponding forwarding physical port	CN111884922-A	The method enables providing simple software processing logic, short cycles, less demand for platform and resources, low impact and avoiding a need of software to maintain MAC address forwarding tables and encapsulation/ decapsulation operations.
Method for cross-device interaction; involves using the first device to determines the user identity of the first device, which is the same as the user identity of the second device; first device is provided to obtained related task information	CN111523095-A	The method avoids searching the target user on the first application of the first device using the user of the first device and improves user convenience of cross-device interaction.
Method for facilitating cross-device and cross-channel advertising and remarketing; involves sending instructions to user's mobile device and wearable electronic device with processor when instruction presents advertisement to user	US2016379245-A1; US10229429-B2	The method enables providing swift elasticity capabilities that can be rapidly and elastically provisioned automatically and to quickly scale out and rapidly release to quickly scale in.

(Continued)

56 Search Support Techniques and Systems

TABLE 4.2 (Continued)

Patent	Patent number	Advantages
Data fusion-based cross–device network information searching system; has search data processing module for searching search results generated by user on device based on data fusion and combined with reordering of device information	CN107273427-A;CN107273427-B	The system avoids repeated information searching time so as to improve searching efficiency and user's searching experience.
Cross-device image file processing method; involves searching human machine interaction interface of image file according to IP interface, and performing remote image extraction operation by IP interface based on click operation response	CN104090877-A; US2014337744-A1; WO2014180200-A1; US9501500-B2; CN104090877-B	The method enables simply and quickly extracting the image from the image file across an inner part of the local area network.

4.3 Cross-device Search-Related Algorithms

The implementation of cross-device search is a complex and systematic process, and the underlying support algorithms are also complex and diverse. Based on the basic process of cross-device search, we can divide the algorithms designed for cross-device search into three categories according to their functions: cross-device user tracking, searching, and recommendation.

Table 4.2 lists some algorithms related to cross-device search, as well as their goals and key features.

4.4 Cross-device Search Systems Introduction and Development

In this section, we introduced the existing the cross-device search-related information systems.

In our previous research, we developed a cross-device search system based on previous research findings and the characteristics of cross-device search. The name of this system is "Cross-device Access and Fusion Engine, CAFE" (https://crosssearch.whu.edu.cn/), and the login page and search result page of CAFE on the desktop is shown in Figure 4.2. This system can help users recall or restore previous search tasks on different devices, and provide recommendations for users. This system is also used in the research of this book.

In previous research, we studied how to improve search technology by perceiving user context in a complex search environment. We proposed a multidimensional

Search Support Techniques and Systems **57**

TABLE 4.2 Cross-device related algorithms

Category	Name	Goals	Key features	Reference
User tracking	AdaBoost classification algorithm	Cross-device tracking	Typing duration; accelerometer in tap	Yuan, Maple, Chen, and Watson (2018)
Searching	Page Rank	Organize search results pages	Web influence; Number of links; Probability access from links	—
	WPR	Optimize page ranking results	Link weight; Number of internal links	Xing and Ghorbani (2004)
	HITS	Search page results ranking	Web page authority score; Web center score; Forwarding page; Reference page	—
	CLEVER	Search page results ranking	Page links	Chakrabarti et al. (1999)
Recommendation	PMI algorithm	Search results recommendation	Query; Web keywords	Deepak, Priyadarshini, and Babu (2016)
	QRM algorithm	Query recommendation	Query-level utility User perceived utility	Wang, Huang, Guo, and Lan (2015)
	QRA based on complex tasks	Query recommendation	Subtask recognition; Subtask merging; Page rank score	Zhao, Zhang, Zhang, Gao, and Li (2018)

user data collection technology, which collects users' multi-touch information on mobile devices, the corresponding search content, and other rich interaction scenarios that carry out in-depth analysis and aggregation and provide support for cross-device search. The comprehensive interactive context model can identify the user's search strategy and search environment, and generate recommended search results for users based on different search intentions and contexts. The reasoning of the search strategy is mainly through the integration of search content information (search questions, click files) and user behavior obtained from the multi-touch information of mobile devices (simple behaviors such as query and click, complex behaviors such as different speeds of up and down drag or zoom in, zoom out, etc.). This is the design idea and framework of the CAFE system, as shown in Figure 4.3.

58 Search Support Techniques and Systems

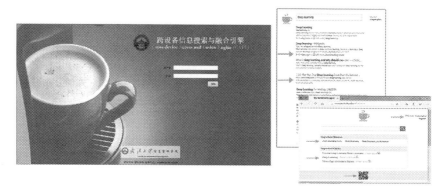

FIGURE 4.2 The login page and search result page of CAFE

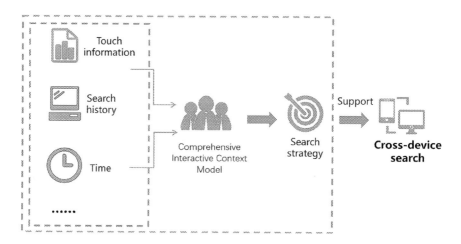

FIGURE 4.3 The design idea of CAFE

To support users' search tasks in a cross-device context, we propose technology that re-ranks search results, based on the original search engine results ranking and integrating users' interactive data in a cross-device context.

This technology not only integrates the traditional search engine document and query matching but also includes the context characteristics of users' cross-device search in the ranking of search results, which can improve users' cross-device searching, improve users' search efficiency, and optimize the user experience, as shown in Figure 4.4.

4.5 Summary

In this chapter, we introduced the existing techniques and systems for cross-device search. We first gave a brief review in the domain of cross-device search

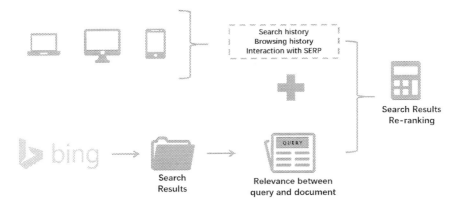

FIGURE 4.4 The search results re-ranking of CAFE

systems. Then, we introduced the cross-device search algorithms in existing studies, including user tracking algorithms, searching-related algorithms, and recommendation algorithms. The implementation of cross-device search is a complex and systematic process, and the underlying support algorithms are also complex and diverse. Following this, we introduced the Cross-device Access and Fusion Engine, a self-developed cross-device search engine. This search engine can utilize user behavior data, such as mobile touch interaction, click-through data, and contextual information, to support users' cross-device searching. This chapter introduced the related research of cross-device search from the perspective of system and technology to enable readers to have a deeper understanding of cross-device search.

Reference

Andolina, S., Klouche, K., Ruotsalo, T., Floréen, P., & Jacucci, G. (2018). Querytogether: Enabling entity-centric exploration in multi-device collaborative search. *Information Processing & Management*, 54(6), 1182–1202.

Brookman, J., Rouge, P., Alva, A., & Yeung, C. (2017). Cross-device tracking: Measurement and disclosures. *Proceedings on Privacy Enhancing Technologies*, 2(2017), 133–148.

Chakrabarti, S., Dom, B. E., Kumar, S. R., Raghavan, P., Rajagopalan, S., Tomkins, A., ... & Kleinberg, J. (1999). Mining the Web's link structure. *Computer*, 32(8), 60–67.

Chang, T. H., & Li, Y. (2011). Deep shot: A framework for migrating tasks across devices using mobile phone cameras. In *Proceedings of the SIGCHI Conference on Human Factors in Computing Systems* May 7 (pp. 2163–2172). Vancouver, Canada.

Deepak, G., Priyadarshini, J. S., & Babu, M. H. (2016, October). A differential semantic algorithm for query relevant web page recommendation. In *2016 IEEE International Conference on Advances in Computer Applications (ICACA)* (pp. 44–49). IEEE. Tamilnadu, India.

Donato, D., Bonchi, F., Chi, T., & Maarek, Y. (2010). Do you want to take notes? Identifying research missions in Yahoo! Search Pad. In *Proceedings of the 19th International Conference on World Wide Web* April 26 (pp. 321–330). Raleigh, USA.

Gomes, S., & Hoeber, O. (2021, March). Supporting cross-session cross-device search in an academic digital library. In *Proceedings of the 2021 Conference on Human Information Interaction and Retrieval* (pp. 337–341). Canberra, Australia

Han, S., Yue, Z., & He, D. (2015). Understanding and supporting cross-device web search for exploratory tasks with mobile touch interactions. *ACM Transactions on Information Systems, 33*(4), 1–34. doi:10.1145/2738036

Morris, D., Ringel Morris, M., & Venolia, G. (2008, April). SearchBar: a search-centric web history for task resumption and information re-finding. In *Proceedings of the SIGCHI Conference on Human Factors in Computing Systems* (pp. 1207–1216). Florence, Italy: ACM

Neufeld, E. (2017). Cross-device and cross-channel identity measurement issues and guidelines: How advertisers can maximize the impact of an identity-based brand campaign. *Journal of Advertising Research, 57*(1), 109–117.

Nikiforakis, N., Kapravelos, A., Joosen, W., Kruegel, C., Piessens, F., & Vigna, G. (2013, May). Cookieless monster: Exploring the ecosystem of web-based device fingerprinting. In *2013 IEEE Symposium on Security and Privacy* (pp. 541–555). IEEE. San Francisco, USA.

Potter, S., & Nieh, J. (2005, May). Webpod: Persistent web browsing sessions with pocketable storage devices. In *Proceedings of the 14th International Conference on World Wide Web* (pp. 603–612). Chiba, Japan.

Wang, J., Huang, J. Z., Guo, J., & Lan, Y. (2015). Recommending high-utility search engine queries via a query-recommending model. *Neurocomputing, 167*, 195–208.

Xing, W., & Ghorbani, A. (2004, May). Weighted pagerank algorithm. In *Proceedings. Second Annual Conference on Communication Networks and Services Research* (pp. 305–314). IEEE. Fredericton, Canada.

Yuan, H., Maple, C., Chen, C., & Watson, T. (2018). Cross-device tracking through identification of user typing behaviours. *Electronics Letters, 54*(15), 957–959.

Zhao, Y., Zhang, Y., Zhang, B., Gao, K., & Li, P. (2018). Recommending queries by extracting thematic experiences from complex search tasks. *Entropy, 20*(6), 459.

Zimmeck, S., Li, J. S., Kim, H., Bellovin, S. M., & Jebara, T. (2017). A privacy analysis of cross-device tracking. In *26th {USENIX} Security Symposium ({USENIX} Security 17)* (pp. 1391–1408).

5

CROSS-DEVICE SEARCH BEHAVIORS

5.1 Related Work on Cross-device Search Behaviors

5.1.1 Multi-session and Cross-session Search Behaviors

Multi-session and cross-session searches can be regarded as a series of queries corresponding to a distinct high-level information need that are segmented into short time units. Cross-device search can be regarded as a special case of cross-session search, generated with the development of personal device ecosystems. A cross-device search consists of a pre-switch session and a post-switch session; in other words, at least two sessions are conducted on separate devices. Therefore, we reviewed studies on multi-session and cross-session searches, which are relevant to cross-device search.

A very early study related to multi-session and cross-session search can be dated back to Spink. Spink (1996) interviewed end-users about their interactions with online public access catalogs (OPAC) and CD-ROM databases over multiple search sessions. Results revealed a common phenomenon: users with a broad problem-at-hand repeatedly seek information in stages over extended periods from a variety of digital information resources. Users tend to use the same or different databases to search pieces of literature to answer the same or evolving problems-at-hand. As time progresses, as the situational context changes, or as the users learn and clarify their question-in-mind, they return to information retrieval systems and conduct more searches. This phenomenon of repeatedly searching over time in relation to the same or evolving information problem is defined as the successive search phenomenon in Spink's subsequent exploration (Spink, Bateman, & Griesdorf, 1998; Spink, Griesdorf, & Bateman, 1999; Spink, Wilson, Ford, Foster, & Ellis, 2002). These studies identify the frequency

DOI: 10.4324/9780429201677-5

62 Cross-device Search Behaviors

of successive searches of different topics, the reasons for successive searches, and changes of terms and databases in successive searches.

Lin and Belkin (2000) were also interested in the successive search phenomenon. Their study proposes a multidimensional conceptual model called "Multiple Information Seeking Episode (MISE)," explaining why and how people search for essentially the same information problem across multiple episodes in terms of four dimensions: problematic situation, information problem and its treatment, information seeking process, and episode. The original model was developed based on a literature review and was further validated by a hybrid study of a controlled experiment and critical incident recall (Lin & Belkin, 2005). The structure of MISE was revised to become an interaction-centered model, comprising factors on both searcher and system sides that could affect successive searches, including six classes of successive search experience: searchers, search activity, search context, information attainment, information use activities, and systems. Afterwards, a deep investigation of the newly revised MISE model was conducted to explore the internetworking factors in the model (Lin, 2005); specifically, how the factors evolve over sessions and how they are affected by other factors.

To deepen the understanding of successive searches, Lin and Xie (2013) quantitatively examined observable behavioral characteristics of successive searches. They focused on one scenario of successive searches, known as transmuting successive searches, in which searchers learn about and gradually refine their information problems during the course of an information search. The results of this study strengthen the validity of the MISE model. One of the most recent studies on cross-session search (Li, Capra, & Zhang, 2020) also investigates the motivations of cross-session search and refers back to the eight renewal modes concluded in the MISE model.

Task interruption and re-finding are common in multi-/cross-session search (Morris, Morris, & Venolia, 2008). Previous research shows that 40% of individuals' information tasks could not be completed in one session, mainly as a result of interruptions (Sellen, Murphy, & Shaw, 2002). People tend to rebuild their memory of the search by re-finding. Existing studies present various concepts associated with re-finding, such as re-search, re-retrieval, re-access, and revisit. Re-access and revisit refer to seeking the URL previously visited, while re-search and re-retrieval indicate re-issuing queries to revisit a web page or to find new websites. Tyler and Zhang (2012) classified types and intentions of re-search. Re-finding prediction can be used to re-rank search results, which improves the retrieval performance of the personalized search. Experiments have shown that ranking relevant URLs with higher re-finding probabilities helps improve NDCG (Normalized Discounted Cumulative Gain), compared with just re-ranking URLs by relevance (Tyler, Wang, & Zhang, 2010).

In recent years, an extension of multi-session search, i.e., multi-session tasks, has been widely studied (Alhenshiri, Walters, Shepherd, & Duffy, 2012; MacKay & Watters, 2012), especially in terms of work tasks. Liu and Belkin (2015) found that in a multi-session task, documents with a longer total dwell time are more

Cross-device Search Behaviors **63**

likely to be useful. Users' knowledge generally increases after each session and there is a ceiling effect, which means that users with high levels of baseline knowledge may not achieve a higher level after multi-session tasks (Liu, Belkin, Zhang, & Yuan, 2013).

Meanwhile, cross-session search detection has drawn researchers' interest. Cross-session search detection can be divided into identifying queries on the same task and predicting task continuation (Agichtein, White, Dumais, & Bennet, 2012; Kotov, Bennett, White, Dumais, & Teevan, 2011). Machine learning methods are used to model cross-session search behavior. Cross-session search behaviors have been actively studied to identify cross-session search tasks. Wang, Song, Chang, and Chu (2013)) developed a semi-supervised clustering model to extract cross-session search tasks from users' search activities. Features related to the similarity among queries and URLs were given importance in their model. Han, Yue, and He (2015)) found that more queries are issued and more web pages are visited and saved in the first session of a cross-session search than in a cross-device search, while the opposite occurs for landing page dwell time.

5.1.2 Interaction and Search Behaviors in Cross-device Scenarios

The multi-device environment generates cross-device scenarios, and usage of multiple devices has been studied frequently. An early study interviewed academia and industry users to investigate why and how people use multiple devices (Dearman & Pierce, 2008). They found that users' activity could not be associated with a particular device. People actively or forcedly use multiple devices according to the advantages or constraints of these devices. Device use varies by the setting where users perform tasks, and individuals tend to distinguish between devices used at work and those used at home. Search behavior in a multi-device world has also received attention. Cecchinato, Sellen, Shokouhi, and Smyth (2016) discovered that email retrieval is mainly conducted on PCs and laptops rather than smartphones. Device use depends on the type of email that users seek and the users' location. Wu and Bi (2017) discussed the impact of different devices (i.e., mobile phones, tablets, and desktop computers) on search pattern transitions by mining the transaction logs of a university library online public access catalog (OPAC). It was found that search field transition patterns are influenced by the input function and user interfaces of different devices.

Cross-device interaction is one form of multi-device use. Results of a survey about web use on multiple devices shows that users visit the same websites on both mobile devices and PCs, and users are interested in sharing websites across devices (Kane et al., 2009). This finding confirms the intent of cross-device web use. Another survey reveals scenarios in which users would like to perform cross-device interactions. Geronimo, Husmann, and Norrie (2016) report that users are most interested in using cross-device applications when watching YouTube videos and planning a trip. Taking an online course and meeting friends are secondary scenarios for interacting across devices. Image processing is the least likely

64 Cross-device Search Behaviors

scenario for cross-device interaction. Many systems and frameworks have been designed to support cross-device interaction, such as DisplayPointers (Strohmeier, 2015) and YanuX Framework (Santos, Madeira, & Correia, 2018). Turner (2013) innovatively combined gaze with mobile input modalities to enable cross-device interaction between public and personal displays. There are two crucial issues in design solutions for cross-device interaction: information transfer (Sohn et al., 2010; Sohn, Mori, & Setlur, 2010) and user matching (Kim, Kini, Koh, Koh, & Getoor, 2017; Tanielian, Tousch, & Vasile, 2018).

Although cross-device interaction has been studied for some time, cross-device search-related research is relatively new. To our knowledge, research on cross-device interaction with an emphasis on searching was not published until the conference paper by Wang et al. (2013). They defined cross-device search by a 7-tuple set comprising pre-switch and post-switch query, session, and device, and found that one-third of switches involve a location shift and cross-device search users prefer the topics of navigation, image, celebrities, and books. Montañez, White, and Huang (2014) concentrated on device transition in cross-device searches. Probabilities of device transition between PCs, smartphones, tablets, and game consoles show that the most likely transition is tablet to PC. Han, Yue, and He (2015)) explored cross-device search behavior only in the context of mobile-to-desktop web search. They compared behavioral patterns in mobile-to-desktop search and desktop-to-desktop search and found significant differences in terms of information exploration, sense-making, and repetitive behaviors. Han, He, and Chi (2017) used the hidden Markov model (HMM) to model observed cross-device search behaviors in two types of cross-device situations: mobile-to-desktop and desktop-to-desktop. Unlike the above studies focusing on cross-device web search, Wu, Liang, and Bi (2018) were interested in the characteristics of cross-device OPAC searches. The PC-to-PC transition was found most frequently, and a variety of query reformulation patterns during device transitions were identified. More exploration was conducted by Wu's research group to gain a deeper understanding of cross-device search behavior, in terms of users' dynamic change of search performance (Wu & Yuan, 2018), task preparation and resumption in cross-device search (Wu, Dong, Tang, & Capra, 2020), and characteristics of cross-device search tasks (Wu, Dong, & Liu, 2019).

5.2 Cross-device Search Experiment Design

5.2.1 Research Motivation

In Chapter 3, we collected the cross-device search experience of global users, and concluded several reasons for searching the same information problem across multiple devices. The findings inspire us to research the characteristics of cross-device search behaviors driven by different motivations.

Motivation is a concept derived from the subject of psychology, and is widely discussed in the fields of psychology, social science, education, etc. Being an indispensable component of human behavior, motivation cannot be ignored in information-seeking behavior studies. Instead of directly being explored among information science literature, information-seeking motivations have been examined under the label of information need. Taylor's question negotiation framework is regarded as one of the first discussions of information need (Taylor, 1968). His four-level model assumes that when an information seeker communicates with a librarian, the needs go through a transformation as follows: visceral, conscious, formalized, and compromised needs. Referring to visceral needs, the ASK (Anomalous State of Knowledge) theory proposed by Belkin (1980) argues the uncertainty of knowledge is a primary motivator for information seeking. When people perceive there is something they do not know but want to, they will pursue a process of information seeking. in other words, the awareness of incomplete or inadequate knowledge triggers the search activity. The well-known ISP (Information Search Process) model also indicates that uncertainty initiates the information search action (Kuhlthau, 1991). Case (2012) contributes a predominant discussion about motivation through what he refers to as a "motivational puzzle" and connects it to information need. Clearly, motivations have long been researched in the area of information seeking. Thus, it is vital to consider motivations in emerging cross-device search behavior studies.

Search intention is a research topic similar to information-seeking motivation. Both search intention and motivation explain why a user is embarking on a search process. Most research on search intentions prefers to excavate through queries from the perspective of goal achievement. A widely applied classification proposed web searches could be divided into three types: navigational, transactional, and informational (Broder, 2002), showing search intentions by what types of information content users aim to find. Another classic typology of search intention argues that web searching includes four goals: fact-finding, information gathering, browsing, and transactions (Kellar, Watters, & Shepherd, 2007).

Meanwhile, search intentions have been investigated through the topical characteristic of search queries. In other words, search intention is equated to the search topic (Baeza-Yates, Calderón-Benavides, & González-Caro, 2006). To some extent, goals reflect users' search motivations. As Dervin's sense-making theory (Dervin, 1998) agrees, goal achievement partially uncovers the motivational force of information seeking. Additionally, information-seeking motivation has a psychological aspect; for example, cognitive and subjective dimensions. However, the difference between search intent and motivation becomes ambiguous, according to a recent paper, where information-seeking intention is deemed a cognitive-level component of search tasks (Liu, Mitsui, Belkin, & Shah, 2019).

Intentions and motivations have been explored in various search contexts. Soleymani, Riegler, and Halvorsen (2017) automatically recognized users' image search intentions using the visual content of the images, user interactions, and spontaneous responses. Tso, Yau, and Cheung (2010) found the intention to change a job is a partial mediator of job search behaviors via motivation. An analysis highlighted five motivations for self-search: as a form of identity

66 Cross-device Search Behaviors

management, to discover reactions to and reuse user-generated media, to re-find personal content, as a form of entertainment, and to reveal lost or forgotten content (Marshall & Lindley, 2014). Among these studies, motivations are inevitably correlated with search behaviors. However, search behaviors under different motivational scenarios have rarely been studied in the situation of cross-device search. The current study of this manuscript aims to fill this gap. Different motivations can provide concrete contextual situations, where we gain a deeper understanding of cross-device search behavior.

5.2.2 Theoretical Background

Self-determination theory (SDT) was introduced in the current research design. SDT was first proposed by Ryan and Deci (2000) and has been well developed over two decades. It consists of six mini-theories: Cognitive Evaluation Theory (CET), Organismic Integration Theory (OIT), Causality Orientations Theory (COT), Basic Psychological Needs Theory (BPNT), Goal Contents Theory (GCT), and Relationships Motivation Theory (RMT).

Ryan and Deci published the latest paper on SDT in the journal where the theory was first published, reviewing and discussing the broad framework of SDT (Ryan & Deci, 2020). SDT suggests individuals are moved to act due to the inherent need for growth and the satisfaction of three types of basic psychological need: autonomy, competence, and relatedness. Autonomy refers to a sense of initiative and ownership over one's actions. People desire to feel in control of their own behaviors and goals. Autonomy is supported by experiences of interest and value, and undermined by experiences of being externally controlled by rewards or punishments. For example, a man with a cold will not see a doctor when he believes it can get well on his own. Competence indicates a sense that one can succeed and grow. People are likely to take action when they feel that they have the skills needed to succeed or achieve their goals. For example, a student will want to join a talent show if he feels he is good at playing the piano. Relatedness indicates a sense of belonging and connection to other people. For example, a child will be willing to sleep in the dark if she knows her parent is nearby.

SDT argues there are three types of motivation: intrinsic motivation, extrinsic motivation, and amotivation. In the realm of SDT, intrinsic motivation is the core. Intrinsic motivation comes from within, and refers to engaging in behavior due to internal drives such as the pleasure, enjoyment, and satisfaction that the behavior provides. Extrinsic motivation involves engaging in behavior due to external sources and rewards that are separable from the behavior itself (Deci & Ryan, 1985; Ryan & Deci, 2000). People experiencing extrinsic motivation might feel pressured or forced to conduct their behavior by external sources.

SDT further differentiates extrinsic motivation by classifying it into four subtypes, ranging across different levels of autonomy: external regulation, introjected regulation, identified regulation, and integrated regulation. External regulation is exclusively external and regulated by externally-imposed rewards and punishments, which is experienced as controlled and non-autonomous. Introjected regulation concerns behavior that is regulated by the internal rewards of self-esteem for success and by avoidance of anxiety, shame, or guilt of failure. It is the form of extrinsic motivation that has been partially internalized, and is also regarded as a controlled motivation. Identified regulation is an autonomous form of extrinsic motivation, suggesting that external pressure has become a personally important self-desired goal. Integrated regulation has the highest level of autonomy, in which people recognize and identify the value of a behavior and deeply internalize it into their own value system.

Amotivation is the form of motivation that lacks intentionality. People do not recognize the connection between their behavior and its outcome, thus having no interest in the behavior they are engaged in (Ryan & Deci, 2020; Savolainen, 2018).

The variations of autonomy existing in motivation introduce another important distinction in the types of motivation: autonomous motivation and controlled motivation. Autonomous motivation consists of motivation from internal sources (i.e., intrinsic motivation), as well as motivation from external sources, where individuals identify the value of behavior and align it with their sense of self (e.g., identified regulation and integrated regulation). Controlled motivation includes external regulation and introjected regulation, which are fully and moderately controlled, respectively. On the one hand, when individuals are motivated by autonomous motivation, they may feel self-directed and autonomous. On the other hand, when individuals are motivated by controlled motivation, they may feel pressured to act in a certain way and experience little to no autonomy (Deci & Ryan, 2008).

Although there is a great deal of information-behavior-related research referencing SDT, it has been applied in only a few studies related to information-seeking behavior. A very early study is a qualitative case study of motivations regarding job information seeking behavior (Savolainen, 2008). Content analysis was conducted based on three types of motivation proposed by SDT: autonomous motivation, controlled motivation, and amotivation. It was found that information seeking involving autonomous motivation is experienced as interesting and enjoyable because it is driven by personal interests and curiosity. Information seeking driven by controlled motivation is stressful because it purposes to comply with internal needs and external requirements.

Using SDT as a theoretical framework, a scale was developed to measure information-seeking motivation, and it was validated in higher education settings (Dubnjakovic, 2017). This measurement instrument consists of three motivational dimensions (amotivation, controlled motivation, and self-determined motivation), based on the motivation taxonomy of SDT (amotivation, extrinsic motivation, and intrinsic motivation). A study focusing on autonomous information seeking found a positive relationship between basic psychological needs and autonomous motivation, confirming that intrinsically motivated individuals invest more effort in information seeking and enjoy it more (Dubnjakovic, 2018).

68 Cross-device Search Behaviors

The utilization of SDT was compared with another psychological theory of motivation, the expectancy-value theory, in order to examine the motivator of information seeking (Savolainen, 2018). SDT is used to investigate the motivator from the perspective of meeting the needs of autonomy and competence. At the same time, expectancy–value theory approaches the motivator by examining the individual's beliefs related to intrinsic enjoyment, attainment value, utility value, and relative cost of information seeking.

In this chapter, cross-device search is discussed in the context of specific motivations, which involves the classification of search motivations. The core point of view of SDT is that human behavior stems from different types of motivation. Unlike other theories of motivation, SDT emphasizes the type of motivation rather than the degree of motivation, which makes SDT suitable for this study. The three representative categories of motivation in SDT (intrinsic motivation, extrinsic motivation and amotivation) are widely applied in the research of user behavior motivation. This classification framework reflects whether users' motivators are endogenous (e.g. values) or exogenous (e.g. rewards and punishments). However, the motivation discussed in this chapter is specifically search motivation, which is generated from information needs and is more inclined to SDT's view than behaviors generated when individuals' autonomous psychological needs are satisfied. Therefore, this chapter adopts the motivation classification proposed by SDT according to the difference of autonomy, namely, autonomous motivation and controlled motivation.

5.2.3 Simulating Cross-device Search Motivations

A crowdsourcing survey of cross-device searching in a real situation uncovered five major reasons that individuals switch devices while searching, including:

- A planned cross-device search ("Planned"), where the user expects to use different devices before performing the search.
- Unsatisfied information needs ("Unsatisfied"), where the user does not obtain the needed information on the anterior device.
- Helping memory ("Memory"), where the user searches on the posterior device in order to remember what he/she has seen on the anterior device.
- Forced to interrupt the search ("Forced"), where the search on the anterior device is suddenly interrupted, so the user has to resume the search on another device.
- Complementing existing search results ("Complement"), where the user expects to acquire more information by searching on another device, even if he/she has found the information needed on the anterior device.

These five reasons provide concrete motivational contexts that lead to cross-device searches, which inspires the current study to explore the differences of cross-device search behavior under various motivations. Since it is difficult to

Cross-device Search Behaviors **69**

simulate the Unsatisfied motivation in a controlled experimental setting, only four reasons were included in the current study (Planned, Memory, Forced, and Complement).

On one hand, Planned and Forced are opposite motivations. The difference exists in whether the searcher knows that there will be an interruption during the process and multiple devices will be used to search. The individual with Planned motivation is aware of a cross-device search in advance, and that the search will be interrupted by the activity of switching devices. In contrast, the individual with Forced motivation does not realize he/she has to change devices until the search is interrupted in the middle of the process. According to SDT, Planned and Forced are considered to be controlled motivations. In the case of Planned motivation, an individual's search behavior is driven by an external factor which is the access to use another device. In the case of Forced motivation, an individual's search behavior is also driven by an external factor which is the interrupted search process. Planned motivation users foresee that multiple devices are available and want to leverage the strength of different devices to achieve a successful search. The search behaviors of Forced motivation users are regulated by the avoidance of anxiety, shame, or guilt for failure to complete the search.

On the other hand, Memory and Complement are contrary to each other. The distinction lies in whether the searcher wants to obtain additional information or knowledge. The individual with Memory motivation purposes to search the information that has been found on the previous device. Contrarily, the individual with Complement motivation is driven to search on another device in order to find more information. Memory and Complement are deemed to be autonomous motivations suggested in SDT. Individuals with both Memory and Complement motivations are encouraged to search due to the desire for knowledge, regardless of their prior knowledge. A desire for knowledge could be generated from the individual's intrinsic motivation or triggered by external sources, such as instructions.

In summary, the current study involves two dimensions of motivation: controlled motivation and autonomous motivation. Controlled motivation includes Planned and Forced, while autonomous motivation includes Memory and Complement. The matrix in Table 5.1 shows four different search motivation scenarios, which the current study designed to analyze the characteristics of cross-device search behavior. We divided participants into two groups. One is

TABLE 5.1 Designed scenarios of cross-device search motivation

Dimension		Controlled motivation	
		Planned	Forced
Autonomous Motivation	Memory Complement	Planned-Memory (P-M) Planned-Complement (P-C)	Forced-Memory (F-M) Forced-Complement (F-C)

70 Cross-device Search Behaviors

the Planned group, where participants were told at the beginning that they would be interrupted to change devices during the search. In this case, participants foresaw a cross-device search. The other is the Forced group, where participants were interrupted to change devices in the middle of searching without being notified in advance. In this case, participants were forced to engage in a cross-device search. To simulate the Memory and Complement motivations, we gave participants different instructions when they were required to switch devices. The instruction for the Memory motivation asked participants to recall what they had searched on the previous device. The instruction for the Complement motivation asked participants to search for more relevant information. The following section introduces details of the entire experimental procedure.

5.2.4 Experiment Procedure

Cross-device searching in the current study indicates the search activity across different devices, excluding self-transition. The device transition directions of the experiment include both desktop-to-mobile and mobile-to-desktop. We rotated the device transition direction among the participants to avoid its influence on search behaviors. The device transition direction could be regarded as a black box in a follow-up analysis, because no matter what the motivation was, the search involved two transition directions. The laptop and smartphone used in the experiment were provided by the researchers.

The current study focuses on the effect of search motivation on cross-device search behavior. All participants were required to search for the same task. We designed the search task according to the results of the crowdsourcing survey on cross-device search experiences, reported in Chapter 3. It was reported the top three subjects of cross-device search are Arts, Shopping and Reference. Considering the participant recruitment would be conducted among university students, we selected Education as the subject of the search task, which is the secondary category of Reference.

According to the statistical test results, the *Subject* of the search task has a significant correlation with the *Complexity of Knowledge Dimension*, the *Complexity of Cognitive Dimension, Environment*, and *Device Switch*. Since the experiment took place in a lab setting and the device transition direction was determined, the search task design did not take the features of *Environment* and *Device Switch* into consideration. The co-occurrences between search subjects and task complexity showed the most likely subject of the complexity "factual knowledge" includes Reference, and Reference is likely associated with the complexity of "understand." Based on the task designing method proposed in Section 3.4.2, we designed the search task depending on the features of the subject of Education, the knowledge complexity of "factual knowledge" and the cognitive complexity of "understand."

Factual knowledge refers to the basic elements that a learner must know to understand a subject or solve a problem; in other words, the knowledge of

Cross-device Search Behaviors   71

TABLE 5.2 Content of the search task and instructions

Category	Content
Search task	You are preparing for the entrance exam of a Master program of Law, so you want to search for information related to the exam. What schools are recruiting students for the Master program of Law? Select two schools and search for how many students are enrolled this year. What are the reference books for the exam? What are the admission scores for the last three years?
Instruction for Memory motivation (I-m)	Please search to recall the information you found before.
Instruction for Complement motivation (I-c)	Please search for information about more schools, in addition to the two you already searched.

"know-what." As for the complexity of "understand," Kelly, Arguello, Edwards, and Wu (2015) distinguished the complexities of cognition from two dimensions of outcome and mental activity. "Understand" tasks require the searcher to identify a list or factors in an information source, and possibly compile the list from multiple sources if a single list cannot be found. The description of the search task is shown in Table 5.2, as well as that of the instructions. As mentioned above, we used different instructions to simulate the motivations of Memory and Complement. The search task and instructions were provided in Chinese during the experiment since the participants were all native Chinese speakers.

When the recruitment was completed, participants were randomly assigned to the groups of Forced and Planned motivations and were randomly provided with the instructions for Memory and Complement motivations. Thus, we had two user groups: the Forced group and the Planned group, each of which included participants engaging in either the instruction for Memory motivation or the instruction for Complement motivation. The whole process of the cross-device search experiment is presented in Figure 5.1

The experiment consisted of five stages: the pre-search, pre-switch search, interruption, post-switch search, and the post-search.

At the pre-search stage, participants were told that the experiment consisted of searching a task, filling in two questionnaires, and answering some interview questions. In addition, we told participants that search behaviors would be logged by the search system and the eye-tracker, and interviews would be recorded. We promised to protect the confidentiality of personal information and asked the participants to sign an agreement. After the brief introduction of the experiment, the participant was shown a printed search task. Participants were told they would need to orally recall the process when finishing the search in order to ensure that the participants took the search seriously.

Then, participants were interviewed for Q1 and asked to complete a pre-test survey. Next, for the Forced group, participants started to search. Contrarily,

72 Cross-device Search Behaviors

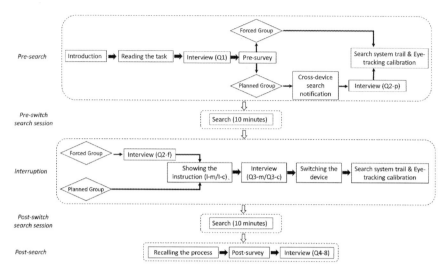

FIGURE 5.1 Experiment procedure

in the Planned group, before starting to search, participants were notified that the search would be a cross-device search, and what the device transition would be. An interview for Q2-p followed. Here, the Forced group had no idea what device would be used to search until we gave it to them. Since a self-developed search system was used, the participant was asked to try it out before starting to search the task. Moreover, a calibration was required by the eye-tracker.

During the pre-switch search stage, the participant searched the task for 10 minutes. The time limit was set to control the total duration of the experiment. Neither the Forced group nor the Planned group was told the time limit. For the Forced group, the search was stopped by the researcher when the time had elapsed. The participants were facing a sudden interruption and being told to change devices. An interview for Q2-f followed. For the Planned group, having been notified at the pre-search stage, participants could foresee an interruption and the device change. Then, participants were shown either the instruction for Memory or the instruction for Complement. An interview for Q3 corresponding to each instruction followed.

After switching devices, participants tried out the search system and had an eye-tracking calibration on the changed device. During the post-switch search stage, the participant continued the search following the given instruction for 10 minutes. Finally came the post-search stage, where the participants briefly recalled the process and took the post-search survey and interview for Q4-8. The survey and interview questions are shown in Section 5.2.6. It took every participant around an hour to complete the process. Participants were rewarded 75 RMB individually.

5.2.5 Participant Demographics

Table 5.3 shows the number of participants involving different scenarios of motivation. The number in each situation is uneven because some recruited people quit for personal reasons, and some people failed to pass the eye-tracker calibration. Finally, valid data of 59 participants remained, whose demographics are reported in Table 5.4. There were 15 males and 44 females, all of whom are under 30 years old. Graduate students accounted for the majority, although students of different education levels were recruited. The majors of the participants vary, including law, engineering, library and information science (LIS), pedagogy, nature science, and literacy. Although the eye-tracker provider declared vision conditions have little impact on tracking performance, we still investigated it; 43 participants are wearing glasses and 16 participants are not.

TABLE 5.3 Participant number of the motivation

Dimension		Controlled motivation	
		Planned	Forced
Autonomous Motivation	Memory	12	16
	Complement	14	17

TABLE 5.4 Demographics of 59 participants

Category	Type	Number
Gender	Male	15
	Female	44
Age	18-25	57
	26-30	2
Education	Undergraduate student	9
	Graduate student	45
	Ph.D student	5
Major	Law	3
	Engineering	2
	LIS	46
	Pedagogy	3
	Nature science	1
	Literary	4
Wearing glasses	Yes	43
	No	16

74 Cross-device Search Behaviors

5.2.6 Data Collection

The study focused on the characteristics of cross-device search behavior under different motivations. To gain a full understanding, it is necessary to collect as many types of behavioral data as possible. As shown in Table 5.5, we collected the data in terms of observable behavioral data, subjective data, and supplementary data.

Specifically, the self-developed search system called Cross-device Access and Fusion Engine (CAFE) was utilized to search and record queries, clicks, cursor movements, and mobile touch interactions (MTI) simultaneously. The CAFE system adopts a context-sensitive retrieval model in accordance with the cross-device search system developed by Han, He, Yue, and Brusilovsky (2015)). The primary interface language of the CAFE system is Chinese. However, like Google, Bing, and other search engines, users can search in multiple languages in CAFE. Search results are in the language consistent with the issued query, and the system prompts are in Chinese. The system provides users with results from Bing re-ranked based on prior interaction data and viewing time. In addition, the system cannot be used to search until users log in, thus enabling users to be uniquely identified in the logs.

During the experiment, each participant was provided with a trial account when trying out the search system and a formal account when starting the search task. The system is available for both desktop and mobile searches. More details about CAFE can be seen in Chapter 4. Specific events of queries, clicks, cursor movements, and MTI are listed in Table 5.6. The "enter" event indicates a query that the user issued to search. Events of click include "click," "page" and "close," indicate the ranking of clicked results on the search engine result page (SERP), the page number of the SERP that the user turns to, and the duration of the page. Events of "cursor," "stay" and "scroll" reflect cursor movements, while the "scroll" event also demonstrates the directions of MTI.

Tobii Pro X3-120 Eye Tracker and Tobii Pro Mobile Device Stand were used to capture participants' gazes during desktop and mobile searches. In the eye-tracking system (i.e., Tobii Studio), a scene camera was set to stimulate the eye tracker, which occurred when the participant visited CAFE's login page. The participant was required to focus on the screen during the search process. The search time of the pre- and post-switch sessions was limited to 10 minutes to

TABLE 5.5 Data types and collecting methods

Aspect	Type	Recording method
Observable behavioral data	Queries, clicks, gazes, cursor movements, & mobile touch interactions (MTI)	CAFE system log, Tobii Pro X3-120 Eye Tracker and Tobii Pro Mobile Device Stand
Subjective data	Familiarity, clarity, difficulty, confidence, & satisfaction	Pre- & Post-survey
Supplementary data	(See interview outlines)	Interview

Cross-device Search Behaviors **75**

TABLE 5.6 CAFE log examples of different events

event_type	event_area	event_content	Note
enter	topBar	法学硕士招生	The user issued a query. Both desktop and mobile.
click	result-title-3		The user clicked the third result on the SERP. Both desktop and mobile.
page	pager->2		The user turned to the second page of the SERP. Both desktop and mobile.
close		18382	The user clicked to close the page, and the duration was 18382 milliseconds. Both desktop and mobile.
cursor		{"cursor":{"last":{"x":715,"y":849},"current":{"x":703,"y":747}}}	Cursor coordinates are recorded every two seconds. By comparing the last and current coordinates, the cursor movements can be known. Desktop only.
stay		{"x":703,"y":747}	If the cursor is static for two seconds, it will be recorded, as well as the coordinates. Desktop only.
scroll		{"scroller":{"last":{"top":976,"left":0},"current":{"top":252,"left":0}}}	Scroller coordinates are recorded every two seconds. By comparing the last and current coordinates, we can know whether the user scrolled up or down, to the left or right. Both desktop and mobile.

TABLE 5.7 Data types of different gaze events

Gaze event	Data type
Fixation	Coordinate, count, duration
Saccade	Count, amplitude
Scan	Length, speed

avoid the impact of fatigue on eye movement. Table 5.7 presents the collected gaze data. Tobii Eye Tracker identified two types of gaze events: fixation and saccade. Fixation count, duration, and location, as well as saccade count and amplitude, were recorded. The saccadic amplitude indicates the distance in visual degrees between the previous fixation location and the current fixation location. According to the coordinates and timestamps of fixations, we identified the scan event and calculated its length and speed.

76 Cross-device Search Behaviors

Subjective data reflects the participants' subjective and cognitive feelings about the cross-device search in terms of familiarity, clarity, difficulty, confidence, and satisfaction. The subjective judgment was measured through a five-level Likert scale, surveyed before and after the search. Questions can be seen in Table 5.8. Measures of familiarity, clarity, and difficulty were repeated in the pre- and post-survey. The feature of confidence measured how well the participant expected to perform. Meanwhile, satisfaction evaluated how well the participant actually performed. Comparing the variations of these measurements under different motivations can reflect the effect of motivation on a cross-device searcher's cognition.

To supplement the explanation of search behaviors, we conducted interviews during the experiment, the questions of which are shown in Table 5.9. Some questions varied among different motivation scenarios. The interviews mainly asked the participants what they thought of different situations during the cross-device search. From the participants' mental activities, we were able to gain insight into their search strategies and cognition of cross-device searching under different motivations.

TABLE 5.8 Questions of pre- & post-surveys

Survey	Question	Measure
Pre	Currently, how familiar do you feel with the search?	Familiarity
	Currently, how clearly do you feel about the search?	Clarity
	Currently, how difficult do you find the search?	Difficulty
	Currently, how confident do you feel about completing the search?	Confidence
Post	Currently, how familiar do you feel with the search?	Familiarity
	Currently, how clearly do you feel about the search?	Clarity
	Currently, how difficult do you find the search?	Difficulty
	Currently, how satisfied do you feel with the search?	Satisfaction

TABLE 5.9 Interview questions

Question	Content	Respondent
Q1	What do you think after reading the search task? (e.g., What do you plan to search next? How are you feeling now? etc.)	All
Q2-p	What do you think about the current situation, where you have been notified you are going to do the cross-device search and the devices you are going to use in sequence? (e.g., What do you plan to search next? How are you feeling now? etc.)	The Planned group

(continued)

Cross-device Search Behaviors **77**

TABLE 5.9 (Continued)

Question	Content	Respondent
Q2-f	What do you think about the current situation, where the search is suddenly interrupted and you have to change devices? (e.g., What do you plan to search next? How are you feeling now? etc.)	The Forced group
Q3-m	What do you think about the current situation, where you are instructed to recall the information you found before? (e.g., What do you plan to search next? How are you feeling now? etc.)	Participants receiving the instruction for Memory (I-m)
Q3-c	What do you think about the current situation, where you are instructed to search for more information? (e.g., What do you plan to search next? How are you feeling now? etc.)	Participants receiving the instruction for Complement (I-c)
Q4	How do you understand the cross-device search?	All
Q5	Considering this experiment experience, how do you think a search engine that supports cross-device search works?	All
Q6	Do you think the interruption and change of devices had any effect on your performance of cross-device searching? Why?	All
Q7-m	When you search across devices to recall information, what do you think search engines should offer to help?	Participants receiving the instruction for Memory (I-m)
Q7-c	When you search across devices to get more information, what do you think search engines should offer to help?	Participants receiving the instruction for Complement (I-c)
Q8	According to the change of measurements in pre- and post-surveys, ask about the reasons for the change.	All

5.2.7 Data Analysis

We explored differences of cross-device search behaviors under various motivations, specifically in terms of queries, clicks, mouse activities, MTI, gazes, and cognition. Multiple measures were utilized to analyze the characteristics of these behaviors. Measures were calculated by the average across all participants, eliminating the influence of the uneven participant number in each motivation.

At first, we compared cross-device search behaviors under different motivations by a descriptive analysis. The comparison was based on the pre-switch search, the post-switch search, and the whole cross-device search process separately. Since there were fewer than 50 participants of each motivation, the Shapiro-Wilk test was performed to estimate normality and to ensure the ANOVA analysis could be applied. Results of $p > 0.05$ indicates normality. Normality test requirements

78 Cross-device Search Behaviors

are usually too strict to be met. Generally, if the absolute value of kurtosis is less than 10 and the absolute value of skewness is less than 3, then the data is basically accepted as a normal distribution. All measures passed the normality test based on this criteria.

A two-way ANOVA analysis was then conducted to statistically test the significance of differences, with the Bonferroni correction procedure to reduce the likelihood of a false positive. The significance was tested based on the whole cross-device search process, because we regarded the device transition direction as a black box. We concentrated on the effect of motivation on the whole search and ignored the influence of device transition directions. Both the interaction effect and the main effect of motivations were discussed. A T-test was further conducted to examine the effect size of the motivation that has major effect on cross-device search behaviors. A qualitative approach of open coding was adopted to analyze the interview transcriptions. We probed for users' search strategies of cross-device search under different motivations.

5.3 Querying in Cross-device Search

5.3.1 Basic Query Characteristics in Cross-device Search

Issuing a query is an essential behavior of cross-device searching, reflecting the user's search intention. For example, query logs could reflect a specific type of medical search intention (White & Horvitz, 2014). Word frequency and query length have been used to classify users' search intentions (Burkhardt, Pattan, Nazemi, & Kuijper, 2017). The connection between queries and intention implies it is necessary to excavate queries when exploring the characteristics of cross-device search behavior under different motivations. In total, 822 queries submitted by 59 participants were collected throughout the experiment. We compared the basic characteristics of the queries in terms of number and length. Specific measures are shown in Table 5.10. We examined the total number of issued queries and unique issued queries separately. Meanwhile, query length was investigated from the aspects of characters and terms.

Figure 5.2 demonstrates the basic query characteristics in the situation of different motivations before and after the user switched search devices. The query number presents a more evident difference among the four situations compared

TABLE 5.10 Measures of basic query characteristics

Measure	Note
QueryNum	The total number of issued queries.
UniQueryNum	The total number of unique issued queries.
AvgCharLength	The average number of characters per issued query.
AvgTermLength	The average number of terms per issued query.

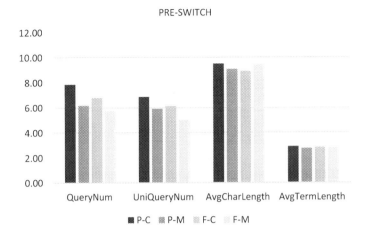

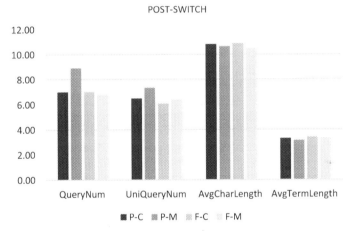

FIGURE 5.2 Basic query characteristics of pre-switch and post-switch searches (Note: P-C refers to Planned-Complement, P-M refers to Planned-Memory, F-C refers to Forced-Complement, F-M refers to Forced-Memory)

with query length. In the pre-switch search, Planned motivation users issued more queries than Forced motivation users. The query number of P-C (7.86) is more than F-C (6.77), and the query number of P-M (6.12) is more than F-M (5.69). The number of unique queries shows a similar trend, where the unique query number of P-C (6.86) is more than F-C (6.12), and the unique query number of P-M (5.92) is more than F-M (5.00).

In the post-switch search, Planned-Memory users submitted the most queries (8.92), clearly more than Planned-Complement users (7.00). The number of unique queries shows a similar trend, where the unique query numbers of P-M and P-C are 7.33 and 6.50 respectively. In contrast, Forced-Memory users (6.75) issued slightly fewer queries than Forced-Complement users (7.00). Meanwhile, the unique query number of F-M (6.38) is more than that of F-C (6.06). It

80 Cross-device Search Behaviors

should also be noted that the query number decreases or remains stable after users switched devices in the situations of P-C and F-C. In contrast, the query number increases in the situations of P-M and F-M. It can be concluded that users tend to issue more queries when they realize there are multiple devices being used or when switching devices to recall the search.

Query length experienced a minor distinction among different motivations. Comparing the pre-switch and post-switch search, the query length of characters and terms both increase after the user switched devices, no matter the situation.

To measure the effect of search motivation on basic query characteristics of cross-device searching, a two-way ANOVA test was conducted, with the controlled (Planned vs. Forced) and autonomous (Complement vs. Memory) motivations as the independent variables. Box plots of measures of query characteristics are shown in Figure 5.3. Over the whole process of cross-device searching, the

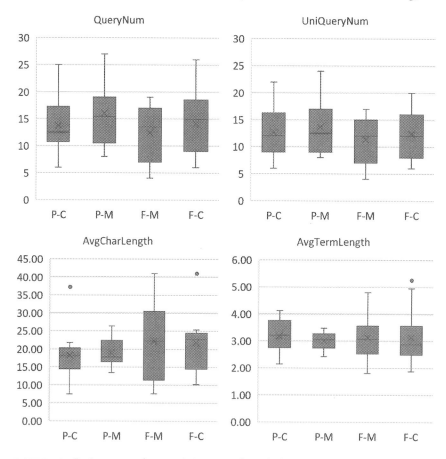

FIGURE 5.3 Basic query characteristics over the whole search (Note: P-C refers to Planned-Complement, P-M refers to Planned-Memory, F-C refers to Forced-Complement, F-M refers to Forced-Memory. The line links the minimum and the maximum. The cross indicates the average.)

Cross-device Search Behaviors **81**

TABLE 5.11 Results of two-way ANOVA on query characteristics

| | Main Effect | | | | | | Interaction Effect | | |
| | Controlled (Planned vs Forced) | | | Autonomous (Complement vs Memory) | | | Controlled ★ Autonomous | | |
	df	F	p	df	F	p	df	F	p
QueryNum	1	1.205	0.277	1	0.051	0.822	1	1.777	0.188
UniQueryNum	1	1.137	0.291	1	0.001	0.972	1	0.668	0.417
AvgCharLength	1	2.444	0.124	1	1.974	0.166	1	0.057	0.812
AvgTermLength	1	0.024	0.877	1	0.016	0.901	1	0.63	0.431

★p < 0.05, ★★p < 0.01

number of both queries and unique queries shows little difference in distribution among different motivations. The query length of both characters and terms experiences either concentrated or scattered distribution, but the average rarely differs. As presented in Table 5.11, there was no significant main effects in query number or query length, and no interaction effects were found between them.

5.3.2 Query Reformulation in Cross-device Search

The process of modifying queries to achieve better search performance is referred to as query reformulation (Jansen, Booth, & Spink, 2009), which is a key component of information seeking. Users express their information needs by constructing and reformulating a series of queries. Driven by various motivations, the user might optimize the queries in different patterns. Research on query reformulation has investigated taxonomies of query refinement. Fidel (1985) categorized query reformulation into operational and conceptual dimensions. Operational reformulation indicates the query is modified, but the meaning is kept the same. Conceptual reformulation refers to refining the query to change its meaning. Rieh and Xie (2006) elaborated on Fidel's taxonomy in three facets of content, format, and resource. They classified query reformulation into four types: specification, generalization, replacement with synonyms, and parallel movement. This classification has been applied and improved in many subsequent studies. On the basis of common terms and differences in two successive queries, Liu, Gwizdka, Liu, Xu, and Belkin (2010) identified five query reformulation types: generalization, specialization, word substitution, repeat, and new. Spelling correction is also identified as a type of query reformulation (Rha, Shi, & Belkin, 2017).

After preliminary analysis of query reformulation activities with our data, we integrated the existing classification of query reformulation, as shown in Table 5.12. Two of the authors coded the query reformulation based on every couple of successive queries in the cross-device search process. Coding reliability

82 Cross-device Search Behaviors

TABLE 5.12 Types of query reformulation

Type	Definition	Cohen's Kappa
Correct	Correcting misspelling of a previous query.	0.84
Generalization	Removing words from a previous query to broaden a search.	0.85
New	Issuing a new query.	0.82
Parallel	The previous queries and the follow-up queries have partial overlap in meaning.	0.94
Repeat	Re-issuing a previously-used query.	0.76
Replacement	Replacing current terms with words that share similar meaning.	0.80
Specification	Adding words to a previous query to narrow down a search.	0.73

was measured by calculating Cohen's Kappa. The overall Cohen's Kappa was 0.85, with all codes achieving a score higher than 0.73 (see Table 5.12). The two coders negotiated each instance of coding difference until an agreement was reached, and then finalized the coding result.

We compared the frequencies of different types of query reformulation among the motivations, as demonstrated in Figure 5.4. In the pre-switch search, Planned motivation users refined queries more frequently than Forced motivation users (12.33 > 10.75). Specifically, Planned motivation users modified more times than Forced motivation users in terms of generalization (1.00 > 0.61), new (2.93 > 2.22), parallel (4.21 > 3.69), replacement (0.71 > 0.42), and specification (2.87 > 2.48). Planned motivation users refined queries less frequently than Forced motivation users in the type of repeat (0.61 < 1.21).

In the post-switch search, Memory motivation users refined queries more frequently than Complement motivation users (15.77 > 13.49), specifically in terms of parallel (7.44 > 4.89) and repeat (2.00 > 1.42). In contrast, Memory motivation users refined queries less frequently than Complement motivation users in types of generalization (0.60 < 0.91), new (2.83 < 3.36), replacement (0.38 < 0.56), and specification (2.19 < 2.34). Moreover, it can be seen that the occurrence of query reformulation increases after the users switched devices, especially for Memory motivation users and in terms of parallel and repeat. This comparison ignores the occurrence of correct since it is too small.

Overall, it was found Planned motivation users modified queries more frequently in the pre-switch search and frequently utilized all types of reformulation but repeat. Meanwhile, Memory motivation users modified queries more frequently in the post-switch search and frequently utilized the patterns of parallel and repeat.

Before conducting the two-way ANOVA test, we examined the frequency of query reformulation in the whole process of cross-device searching. Box plots of reformulation types are presented in Figure 5.5, excluding correct, which rarely occurred. The most popular reformulation pattern in the cross-device search is

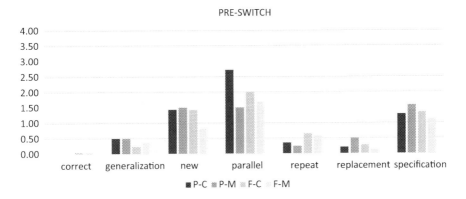

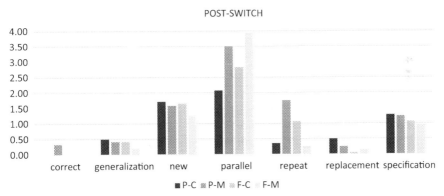

FIGURE 5.4 Query reformulation occurrence of pre-switch and post-switch searches (Note: P-C refers to Planned-Complement, P-M refers to Planned-Memory, F-C refers to Forced-Complement, F-M refers to Forced-Memory)

parallel, followed by new, repeat, and specification. Generalization and replacement are two types that were rarely witnessed. The occurrences of generalization, parallel, new, and specification differ little among different motivations. Meanwhile, the frequencies of repeat and replacement elaborate a clear difference in different motivations. Users in the situations of P-M and F-C modified queries more frequently by issuing repeat queries. Furthermore, replacement pattern was frequently utilized by users in the situations of P-C and P-M.

The ANOVA analysis reveals a significant main effect of controlled motivation (i.e., Planned vs Forced) on the replacement pattern (F = 9.565, p = 0.003 < 0.01). It indicates that, compared with Forced motivation users, Planned motivation users modified queries more frequently by replacing the current query with terms of similar meaning. In addition, as shown in Table 5.13, there is a significant interaction between controlled and autonomous motivations in terms of the repeat pattern (F = 9.985, p = 0.003 < 0.01). It seems the controlled motivation has an impact on the autonomous motivation when users refine queries by repeat pattern. As shown in Figure 5.5, the occurrence of repeat in P-M is

84 Cross-device Search Behaviors

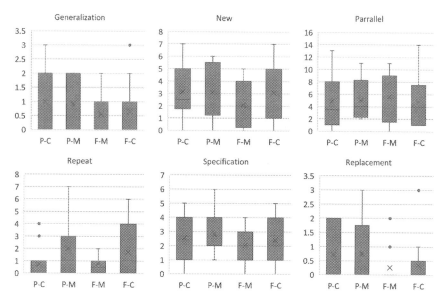

FIGURE 5.5 Query reformulation occurrence over the whole search (Note: P-C refers to Planned-Complement, P-M refers to Planned-Memory, F-C refers to Forced-Complement, F-M refers to Forced-Memory. The line links the minimum and the maximum. The cross indicates the average.)

TABLE 5.13 Results of two-way ANOVA on query reformulation

	Main effect							Interaction effect		
	Controlled (Planned vs. Forced)			Autonomous (Complement vs. Memory)			Controlled * autonomous		
	df	F	p	df	F	p	df	F	p
Generalization	1	3.286	0.075	1	0.002	0.965	1	0.096	0.758
New	1	1.064	0.307	1	0.972	0.329	1	0.765	0.386
Parallel	1	0.108	0.744	1	0.253	0.617	1	0.085	0.772
Repeat	1	0.004	0.951	1	0.508	0.479	1	9.985	0.003**
Replacement	1	9.565	0.003**	1	0.135	0.715	1	0.292	0.591
Specification	1	1.46	0.232	1	0.013	0.91	1	0.63	0.431

*p < 0.05, **p < 0.01

more than P-C (2.00 > 0.25), while the occurrence of repeat in F-C is more than F-M (1.71 > 0.60). When users were notified of a cross-device search in advance, more repeated queries were submitted to help recall the information. On the other hand, when facing an unexpected interruption and being forced to engage in a cross-device search, users would frequently repeat queries to supply the information.

5.3.3 Query Semantics Characteristics in Cross-device Search

Characteristics of query semantics were investigated through the diversity and similarity of query terms. As noted in Table 5.14, we used the query vocabulary richness (QVR) to measure semantic diversity, and the Jaccard similarity coefficient to measure semantic similarity. Referring to Yue, Han, and He (2013), QVR is calculated as:

$$QVR = \frac{T_{Unique\ Terms}}{Q}$$

where $T_{Unique\ Terms}$ refers to the number of unique terms, and Q refers to the number of issued queries.

The Jaccard similarity coefficient is a classic statistic used to measure similarities between sample sets. To measure the semantic similarity of queries in cross-device searches, the Jaccard similarity coefficient was defined as the terms of the intersection divided by the terms of the union of the queries of pre-switch and post-switch sessions:

$$Jaccard\ Similarity = \frac{|T_{pre} \cap T_{post}|}{|T_{pre} \cup T_{post}|}$$

where T_{pre} refers to the number of query terms in the pre-switch session, and T_{post} refers to the number of query terms in the post-switch session. Queries were segmented into terms using Jieba, the Python Chinese word segmentation module.

The calculation of JaccardSimilarity was based on queries during the whole search process, though the QVR was compared between the pre-switch and post-switch searches (see Figure 5.6). In the pre-switch search, Forced motivation users issued more diverse queries than Planned motivation users. It is demonstrated the QVR of F-C is higher than that of P-C (1.50 > 1.37), while the QVR of F-M is higher than that of P-M (1.59 > 1.57). In the post-switch search, queries issued by Complement motivation users varied more than those by Memory motivation users. It can be seen that the QVR of P-C is higher than that of P-M (1.42 > 1.30), while the QVR of F-C is higher than that of F-M (1.67 > 1.56). Moreover, the QVR of P-C and P-M is lower than the QVR of F-C and

TABLE 5.14 Measures of query semantics

Measure	Note
QVR	The average number of unique terms per query.
JaccardSimilarity	Jaccard similarity coefficient of queries between pre-switch and post-switch search sessions.

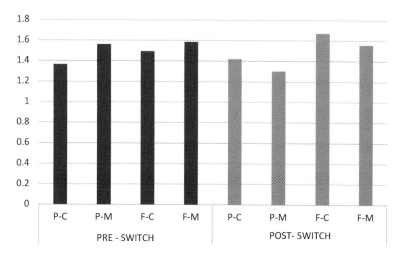

FIGURE 5.6 QVR of pre-switch and post-switch searches (Note: P-C refers to Planned-Complement, P-M refers to Planned-Memory, F-C refers to Forced-Complement, F-M refers to Forced-Memory)

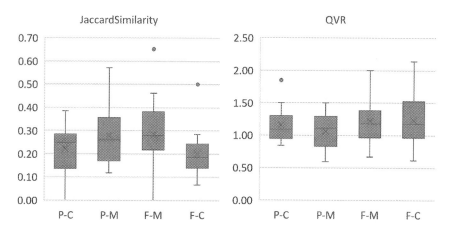

FIGURE 5.7 Query semantics over the whole search (Note: P-C refers to Planned-Complement, P-M refers to Planned-Memory, F-C refers to Forced-Complement, F-M refers to Forced-Memory. The line links the minimum and the maximum. The cross indicates the average.)

F-M, which indicates queries submitted by Forced motivation users vary more than those by Planned motivation users. In summary, users issued queries more distinctively when being forced to perform a cross-device search or aiming to complement the information in a post-switch search.

Figure 5.7 shows the different JaccardSimilarity and QVR of four motivational situations over the whole cross-device search. It can be seen that more

Cross-device Search Behaviors **87**

TABLE 5.15 Results of two-way ANOVA on query semantics

	Main effect						Interaction Effect		
	Controlled (Planned vs. Forced)			Autonomous (Complement vs. Memory)			Controlled ＊ Autonomous		
	dfz	F	p	df	F	p	df	F	p
QVR	1	2.653	0.109	1	0.096	0.758	1	0.028	0.868
JaccardSimilarity	1	1.107	0.297	1	4.992	0.030★	1	0.103	0.75

★p < 0.05. ★★p < 0.01

apparent differences were found in JaccardSimilarity than QVR. The subsequent ANOVA analysis confirms a significant main effect of the autonomous motivation in JaccardSimilarity (F = 4.992, p = 0.30 < 0.05), as seen in Table 5.15. It was found the JaccardSimilarity of the Memory motivation is significantly higher than that of the Complement motivation. It can be concluded that users chose queries that share similar terms to recall information in cross-device searches.

5.4 Clicking in Cross-device Search

5.4.1 Click Behavior Measurement

Clicking is a behavior that cannot be ignored in the study of information seeking. Analysis of click behavior can be widely witnessed in research related to web search ranking (Jain & Varma, 2011), query recommendation (Li, Li, Wu, Zhou, & Wang, 2019), search behavior prediction (Zhang, Chen, Wang, & Yang, 2011), etc. The current study also took click behavior into consideration when we explored characteristics of cross-device search behavior. Click behavior usually reflects searching effectiveness and satisfaction, with a variety of measures being used. It is typical to see click count, click rankings, and SERP depth in search log analysis. An analysis of children's Google search behavior examined the number of results clicked on SERPs, and the rank of the first clicked result (Gwizdka & Bilal, 2017). In addition to the aspect of frequency, click behavior can also be measured considering viewing time (Ellison, Triệu, Schoenebeck, Brewer, & Israni, 2020). Previous studies (Guo & Agichtein, 2010; Sculley, Malkin, Basu, & Bayardo, 2009) proposed the concepts of satisfied clicks and dissatisfied clicks, which were defined by the dwell time on the landing page with 30- and 15-second thresholds. Reviewing the measurement of click behavior, we concluded five measures to analyze click behavior in cross-device searches (see Table 5.16). The analysis only considered clicks on SERPs. There were 1,410 clicks in total collected from both desktop and mobile devices.

88 Cross-device Search Behaviors

TABLE 5.16 Measures of clicks

Measure	Note
ClickNum	The total number of clicks on SERP.
AvgClickDepth	The average of rankings per click.
SatisfiedClick	The number of clicks with a landing page time of at least 30 seconds.
DissatisfiedClick	The number of clicks with a landing page time of at most 15 seconds.
MaxSERPdepth	The maximum page number of SERP.

5.4.2 Click Characteristics during the Cross-device Search

Click behavior under different motivations was compared by the five measures, as seen in Figure 5.8. In the pre-switch search, Planned motivation users performed more clicks than Forced motivation users. It can be seen that the click

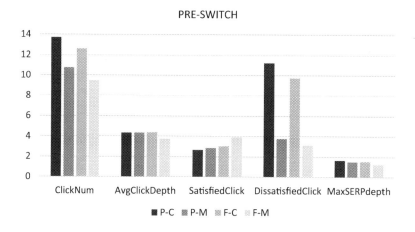

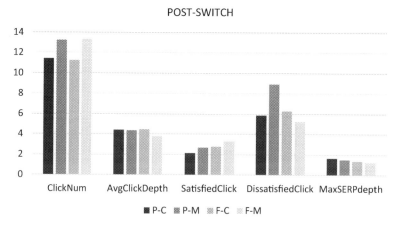

FIGURE 5.8 Click characteristics of pre-switch and post-switch searches (Note: P-C refers to Planned-Complement, P-M refers to Planned-Memory, F-C refers to Forced-Complement, F-M refers to Forced-Memory)

count of P–C is higher than that of F–C (13.71 > 12.59), and the same trend is shown between P–M and F–M (10.75 > 9.50). Dissatisfied clicks are seen more frequently among Planned motivation users than Forced motivation users (P–C = 11.21 > F–C = 9.71 and P–M = 3.75 > F–M = 3.13). The distinction of satisfied clicks between users of Planned and Forced motivations is the opposite. Satisfied clicks are seen less frequently among Planned motivation users than Forced motivation users (P–C = 2.64 < F–C = 3.00 and P–M = 2.83 < F–M = 3.94). Satisfied clicks differ from dissatisfied clicks in the dwell time on a landing page. To conclude, users prefer to quickly view the landing page when planning to search across different devices. No clear difference between the users of Planned and Forced motivations was found in terms of average click depth (P–C = 4.33, F–C = 4.38, F–C = 4.34, F–M = 3.74). For the maximum SERP depth, Planned motivation users clicked a deeper page than Forced motivation users (P–C = 1.64 > F–C = 1.53 and P–M = 1.50 > F–M = 1.25).

In the post-switch search, Memory motivation users clicked more frequently than Complement motivation users (P–M = 13.25 > P–C = 11.43 and F–M = 13.31 > F–C = 11.24). Users in the situation of P–M performed the most dissatisfied clicks (8.92), followed by F–C (6.29), P–C (5.86), and F–M (5.25). In the aspect of satisfied clicks, Memory motivation users clicked more than Complement motivation users (P–M = 2.67 > P–C = 2.14 and F–M = 3.31 > F–C = 2.77). It can be deduced that users tend to carefully view the landing page when searching to remember after a device transition. Differences in average click depth among different motivations were found to be very small (P–C = 4.41, P–M = 4.36, F–C = 4.47, F–M = 3.77). As for the maximum SERP depth, Complement motivation users clicked slightly deeper than Memory motivation users (P–C = 1.64 > P–M = 1.50 and F–C = 1.35 > F–M = 1.25).

Click behavior was further analyzed from the perspective of the whole search process. Figure 5.9 demonstrates the five measures of click behavior over the entire cross-device search. Table 5.17 reports the significant differences of click behavior among the motivations. The main effect of motivation on click behavior during cross-device searching was found. To be concrete, the controlled motivation has a significant impact on the maximum SERP depth ($F = 7.61$, $p = 0.008 < 0.01$). Planned motivation users clicked deeper SERP than Forced motivation users, which indicates that users will view more results if they plan to perform a cross-device search. Moreover, the autonomous motivation significantly influences the average click depth during the cross-device search ($F = 5.939$, $p = 0.018 < 0.05$). Complement motivation users clicked deeper results than Memory motivation users. It is clear that users would like to view more results to acquire additional information.

5.5 Cursor Movements and Touching in Cross-device Search

5.5.1 Desktop Cursor Movements in Cross-device Search

Cross-device searching involves both desktop and mobile search devices. Due to the particularity of the device, some interactions only occur on a certain kind of equipment; on the desktop, this is cursor movement. Cursor movement data

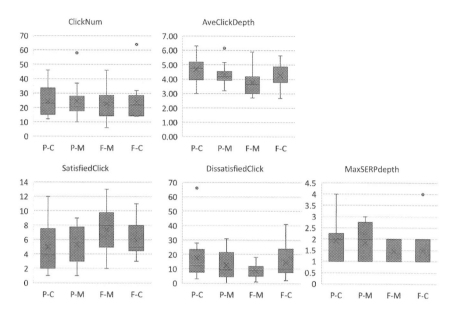

FIGURE 5.9 Click characteristics over the whole search (Note: P-C refers to Planned-Complement, P-M refers to Planned-Memory, F-C refers to Forced-Complement, F-M refers to Forced-Memory. The line links the minimum and the maximum. The cross indicates the average.)

TABLE 5.17 Results of two-way ANOVA on clicks

	Main effect						Interaction effect		
	Controlled (Planned vs. Forced)			Autonomous (Complement vs. Memory)			Controlled * autonomous		
	df	F	p	df	F	p	df	F	p
ClickNum	1	0.159	0.692	1	0.108	0.744	1	0.849	0.361
AvgClickDepth	1	3.356	0.072	1	5.939	0.018★	1	0.003	0.954
SatisfiedClick	1	3.842	0.055	1	1.348	0.251	1	0.523	0.473
DissatisfiedClick	1	0.482	0.49	1	2.356	0.131	1	1.145	0.289
MaxSERPdepth	1	7.61	0.008★★	1	0.007	0.936	1	0.361	0.551

★p < 0.05, ★★p < 0.01

record the positions of users' mouse cursors on the web page of the desktop computer. Cursor movements suggest rich information about users' interactions with the search system, especially when there is no click (Huang, White, & Dumais, 2011). Similar to clicks and gazes, cursor movements are regarded as an implicit indicator of interest in search behavior studies. The correlation between cursor movement and gaze has been studied in depth (Huang, White, & Buscher, 2012).

It has been found that moving the cursor is usually done as a reading aid, which can provide signals about the user's attention. Therefore, cursor movements have been used to understand information-seeking behavior (Youngmann & Yom-Tov, 2018). It is believed that cursor movements can help reveal a searcher's intent; for example, in the case of good abandonment, where a user's information need is satisfied on a SERP with no result being clicked. The relationship between intent and mouse cursor has been investigated (Martín-Albo, Leiva, Huang, & Plamondon, 2016). When a user's intent is clear, the cursor movement is reconstructed almost perfectly, while the reverse is observed when the user's intent is unclear.

In the current study, cursor movements were taken into consideration to understand the differences of cross-device search behavior under different motivations. We examined characteristics of the mouse cursor from two dimensions: frequency and speed. Cursor movement speed indicates the pixel distance of cursor movement divided by the movement duration. Specific measures are listed in Table 5.18, including the cursor movements of different directions.

Analysis of cursor movement frequency and speed of pre-switch and post-switch searches can be seen in Figures 5.10 and 5.11. In the pre-switch search, Planned motivation users moved the cursor more frequently than Forced motivation users, no matter the direction. It is worth noting that Planned motivation users moved the cursor up-left more frequently than Forced motivation users. This suggests that when users expected to use another search device, it would be possible to view back the SERP. For cursor movement speed, Planned motivation users moved the cursor more quickly than Forced motivation users in most directions. The reverse was only observed in the direction of down-right.

In the post-switch search, Memory motivation users moved the cursor more frequently than Complement motivation users. As for the speed, users in the P-M situation moved the cursor more quickly than users in the P-C situation,

TABLE 5.18 Measures of cursor movements

Measure	Note
DownFreq_C	The frequency of cursor movements in different directions.
DownRightFreq_C	
DownLeftFreq_C	
UpFreq_C	
UpRightFreq_C	
UpLeftFreq_C	
DownSpeed_C	The pixel distance per second of cursor movements in different directions.
DownRightSpeed_C	
DownLeftSpeed_C	
UpSpeed_C	
UpRightSpeed_C	
UpLeftSpeed_C	

92 Cross-device Search Behaviors

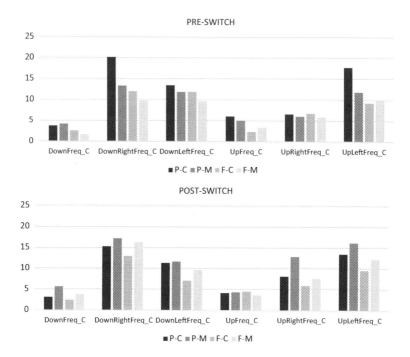

FIGURE 5.10 Cursor movement frequency of pre-switch and post-switch searches (Note: P-C refers to Planned-Complement, P-M refers to Planned-Memory, F-C refers to Forced-Complement, F-M refers to Forced-Memory)

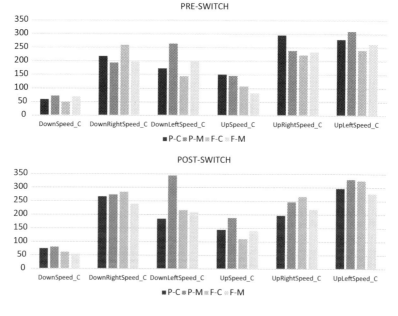

FIGURE 5.11 Cursor movement speed of pre-switch and post-switch searches (Note: P-C refers to Planned-Complement, P-M refers to Planned-Memory, F-C refers to Forced-Complement, F-M refers to Forced-Memory)

Cross-device Search Behaviors **93**

while users in the F–M situation moved the cursor more slowly than users in the F–C situation. Motivated by the demand to search in order to recall, users who expected the device transition viewed the SERP more quickly than those who engaged in an unexpected cross-device search.

According to Table 5.19, the main effect of controlled and autonomous motivations on cursor movements was found. Controlled motivation significantly influenced cursor movements in terms of DownFreq_C (F = 9.485, p = 0.003 < 0.01), DownLeftFreq_C (F = 5.716, p = 0.020 < 0.05), UpFreq_C (F = 5.574, p = 0.022 < 0.05) and UpLeftFreq_C (F = 4.885, p = 0.031 < 0.05). As seen in Figure 5.12, Planned motivation users performed more cursor movements than Forced motivation users in the directions of down, down-left, up, and up-left. Meanwhile, autonomous motivation has a significant impact on the cursor speed moving down-left (F = 8.353, p = 0.006 < 0.01). Quicker cursor movements to down left were observed among Memory motivation users, compared with Complement motivation users.

Also, there is a significant interaction effect on cursor movements between controlled and autonomous motivations, witnessed by the measure of DownRightSpeed_C (F = 4.277, p = 0.043 < 0.05). Users who planned to have a cross-device search moved the cursor down-right more quickly when searching to recall information. Users who were involved in an unexpected cross-device search moved the cursor down-right more quickly when searching to supply information.

TABLE 5.19 Results of two-way ANOVA on cursor movements

| | Main effect | | | | | | Interaction effect | | |
| | Controlled (Planned vs. Forced) | | | Autonomous (Complement vs. Memory) | | | Controlled* autonomous | | |
	df	F	p	df	F	p	df	F	p
DownFreq_C	1	9.485	0.003**	1	1.686	0.2	1	0.012	0.912
DownRightFreq_C	1	1.533	0.221	1	0.354	0.555	1	0.668	0.417
DownLeftFreq_C	1	5.716	0.020*	1	0.024	0.876	1	0.915	0.343
UpFreq_C	1	5.574	0.022*	1	0.223	0.639	1	0.223	0.639
UpRightFreq_C	1	0.512	0.477	1	0.016	0.899	1	0.8	0.375
UpLeftFreq_C	1	4.885	0.031*	1	1.979	0.165	1	0.099	0.755
DownSpeed_C	1	2.116	0.152	1	1.335	0.253	1	0.022	0.884
DownRightSpeed_C	1	1.808	0.184	1	0.733	0.396	1	4.277	0.043*
DownLeftSpeed_C	1	3.819	0.056	1	8.353	0.006**	1	2.415	0.126
UpSpeed_C	1	3.513	0.067	1	0.258	0.614	1	0.328	0.569
UpRightSpeed_C	1	0.684	0.412	1	0.683	0.412	1	0.046	0.832
UpLeftSpeed_C	1	0.359	0.552	1	0.516	0.475	1	1.693	0.199

*p < 0.05, **p < 0.01

94 Cross-device Search Behaviors

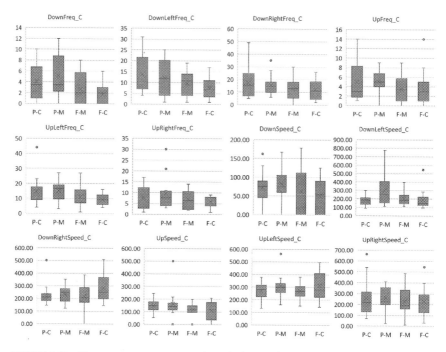

FIGURE 5.12 Cursor movements over the whole search (Note: P-C refers to Planned-Complement, P-M refers to Planned-Memory, F-C refers to Forced-Complement, F-M refers to Forced-Memory. The line links the minimum and the maximum. The cross indicates the average)

5.5.2 Mobile Touch Interactions (MTI) in Cross-device Search

Just as cursor movements are unique interactions on desktops, mobile touch interactions (MTI) are considered unique actions on mobile devices. It is necessary to include MTI in the analysis of cross-device search behavior. Believing that MTI indicates users' implicit search intents, researchers have tried exploiting it to optimize the search experience (Kim, Thomas, Sankaranarayana, Gedeon, & Yoon, 2017; Tran, Trewin, Swart, John, & Thomas, 2013). MTI was found to be an important indicator of document relevance and user satisfaction in web searches (Guo, Jin, Lagun, Yuan, & Agichtein, 2013; Guo, Yuan, & Agichtein, 2011). Inspired by this, Han, Yue, and He (2015)) explored the methods of weighting click-through documents by MTI-based predicted relevance. Like cursor movements discussed above, the current study tries to understand MTI in cross-device searching from the angles of frequency and speed. The measures of MTI are presented in Table 5.20. We examined the frequency and speed of MTI in four directions.

Figures 5.13 and 5.14 show the frequency and speed of MTI in different directions in pre-switch and post-switch searches. It can be seen that the most frequent MTI is swiping up, followed by swiping down and left. In the aspect of speed, the quickest MTI is swiping down, followed by swiping up and left. Swiping

Cross-device Search Behaviors 95

TABLE 5.20 Measures of MTI

Measure	Note
UpFreq_M	The frequency of MTI in different directions.
DownFreq_M	
LeftFreq_M	
RightFreq_M	
UpSpeed_M	The pixel distance per second of MTI in different directions.
DownSpeed_M	
LeftSpeed_M	
RightSpeed_M	

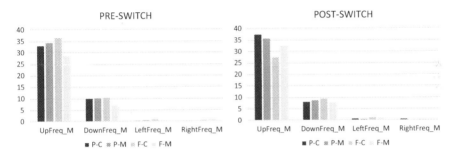

FIGURE 5.13 MTI frequency of pre-switch and post-switch searches (Note: P-C refers to Planned-Complement, P-M refers to Planned-Memory, F-C refers to Forced-Complement, F-M refers to Forced-Memory)

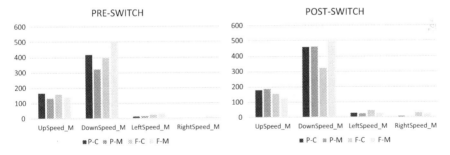

FIGURE 5.14 MTI speed of pre-switch and post-switch searches (Note: P-C refers to Planned-Complement, P-M refers to Planned-Memory, F-C refers to Forced-Complement, F-M refers to Forced-Memory)

right was observed too rarely to make a comparison. In the pre-switch search, users in the situation of F-C swiped up more than users in the situation of P-C, while users in the situation of P-M swiped up more than users in the situation of F-M. Swiping up on the screen indicates the user was looking down on the SERP, which is a typical behavior during searching. There is a clear difference in swiping down between the users in the situations of P-M and F-M. Users in the

96 Cross-device Search Behaviors

situation of P-M performed more swipe-down actions than users in the situation of F-M. Swiping down on the screen indicates the user was reviewing upwards on the SERP. Differences in MTI speed are relatively apparent in swiping down and left. Users in the situation of P-C swiped down quicker than users in the situation of F-C, while users in the situation of F-M swiped down quicker than users in the situation of P-M. As for swiping left, Forced motivation users acted quicker than Planned motivation users. Swiping left on the screen indicates the user was looking to the right on the SERP, which is consistent with the natural reading direction.

In the post-switch search, users in the situation of P-C swiped up more than users in the situation of P-M, while users in the situation of F-M swiped up more than users in the situation of F-C. The reverse was observed in the frequency of swiping down. Users in the situation of P-M swiped down more than users in the situation of P-C, while users in the situation of F-C swiped down more than users in the situation of F-M. In terms of swiping to the left, Complement motivation users acted more than Planned motivation users. Notable differences in MTI speed between users in the situations of F-C and F-M were observed. Users in the situation of F-C swiped up and to the left quicker, while users in the situation of F-M swiped down quicker.

According to Figure 5.15, there are very few occurrences of swiping to the right. Thus, we only conducted the two-way ANOVA analysis on MTIs of up, down, and left (see Table 5.21). It was found the main effect of autonomous motivation on MTI speed was in terms of swiping down ($F = 5.586$, $p = 0.022 < 0.05$) and swiping to the left ($F = 5.645$, $p = 0.021 < 0.05$). Memory motivation users swiped down quicker than Complement motivation users. It can be concluded that searching to recall motivated the user to review upwards on the SERP quickly. On the other hand, Complement motivation users swiped to the left quicker than Memory motivation users. When swiping to the left, users were likely to read the content of a result snippet after zooming in. This indicates that searching to supply information encouraged the users to view the result content quicker.

5.6 Gazing in Cross-device Search

5.6.1 Eye Tracking Analysis of Search Behavior

A large body of literature indicates that eye tracking is conducive to promoting understanding of users' attention, because users' gaze characteristics can show which part of a web page receives more attention (Buscher, Dumais, & Cutrell, 2010; Cutrell & Guan, 2007; Granka, Joachims, & Gay, 2004). Eye tracking involves several aspects with many indicators that can be measured, including fixations, saccades, vergence movements, and so on (Kim, Thomas, Sankaranarayana, Gedeon, & Yoon, 2015). Eye-tracking research methods are widely used to study users' searching behavior. Kim et al. (2015) examined users' search behavior on large and small screens. Eye-tracking data revealed that

Cross-device Search Behaviors **97**

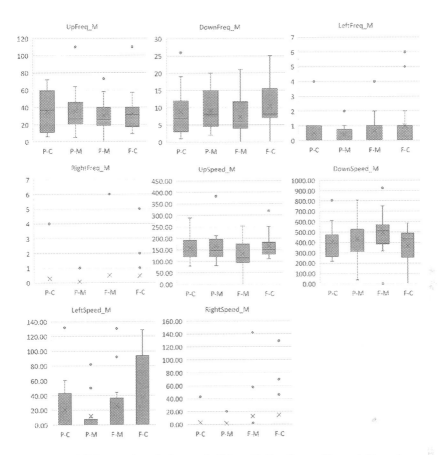

FIGURE 5.15 MTI over the whole search (Note: P-C refers to Planned-Complement, P-M refers to Planned-Memory, F-C refers to Forced-Complement, F-M refers to Forced-Memory. The line links the minimum and the maximum. The cross indicates the average)

TABLE 5.21 Results of two-way ANOVA on MTI

	Main Effect							Interaction Effect		
	Controlled (Planned vs. Forced)			Autonomous (Complement vs. Memory)			Controlled * Autonomous		
	df	F	p	df	F	p	df	F	p
UpSpeed_M	1	0.78	0.381	1	0.514	0.477	1	0.433	0.513
DownSpeed_M	1	0.129	0.721	1	0.207	0.651	1	2.232	0.141
LeftSpeed_M	1	2.414	0.127	1	0.187	0.667	1	0.187	0.667
UpSpeed_M	1	0.448	0.506	1	1.734	0.194	1	0.225	0.637
DownSpeed_M	1	0.507	0.479	1	5.586	0.022★	1	0.739	0.394
LeftSpeed_M	1	2.497	0.121	1	5.645	0.021★	1	1.392	0.244

★$p < 0.05$, ★★$p < 0.01$

98 Cross-device Search Behaviors

TABLE 5.22 Measures of eye movements

Measure	Note
FixationCountPCT	The percentage of fixations on the SERP in fixations of the whole process.
FixationDurationPCT	The percentage of fixation duration on the SERP in fixation duration of the whole process.
AvgSaccadicAmplitude	The average degrees between the previous fixation and the current fixation per saccade.
ScanSpeed	The average pixel distance between the previous fixation and the current fixation per saccade.

it is difficult to extract information from smaller screens, but searching time does not differentiate between large screen searching and small screen searching. Bhattacharya and Gwizdka (2018) used eye-tracking data to show cognitive changes in users. They found that users who obtain more knowledge while searching differ from ones who obtain less knowledge in reading-sequence-length, reading-sequence-duration, and the number of reading fixations. Other studies use eye tracking to analyze certain aspects of search behavior. Through eye-tracking data, Ginsca, Popescu, and Lupu (2015) verified that users are more willing to rely on search engine ranking and are reluctant to choose a result that is ranked lower but is more relevant. Yaneva, Ha, Eraslan, Yesilada, and Mitkov (2018) used eye-movement data to analyze the characteristics of autism retrieval behavior. Kim, Thomas, Sankaranarayana, Gedeon, and Yoon (2016) focused on eye movements during searching on mobile devices. They found that during the retrieval process, users often have fewer eye movements for the top links and tend to select a result for detailed reading after scanning the SERP.

In our cross-device search experiment, we conducted eye tracking on both desktop and mobile devices. The eye-tracking analysis allows us to explore characteristics of cross-device search behavior in the aspect of gaze behavior. In light of the measures of eye movement used in previous studies and the condition of our collected eye-tracking data, four gaze measures were utilized in the current analysis, as shown in Table 5.22. Two main types of gaze events were included: fixation and saccade. Fixations were elaborated on from the aspects of count and duration. Furthermore, we calculated the average amplitude of every saccade. The scanning speed was calculated on the basis of the saccade event.

5.6.2 Characteristics of Eye Movement in Cross-device Search

Figure 5.16 demonstrates characteristics of fixation and saccade in pre-switch and post-switch searches. In the pre-switch search, the Planned motivation users had more fixations than Forced motivation users (P-C = 0.26 > F-C = 0.19 and P-M = 0.25 > F-M = 0.22). Fixation duration shows a similar trend between users of Planned and Forced motivations (P-C = 0.26 > F-C = 0.18 and P-M = 0.24 >

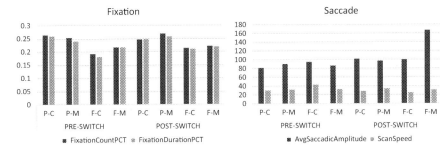

FIGURE 5.16 Eye movements of pre-switch and post-switch searches (Note: P-C refers to Planned-Complement, P-M refers to Planned-Memory, F-C refers to Forced-Complement, F-M refers to Forced-Memory)

F-M = 0.22). Users in the situation of P-M had a larger saccadic amplitude than users in the situation of P-C (90.51 > 81.52). In comparison, users in the situation of F-C had a larger saccadic amplitude than users in the situation of F-M (95.11 > 85.54). Differences in scan speed among different motivations are similar to saccadic amplitude. Users in the situation of P-M scanned a little quicker than users in the situation of P-C (31.86 > 30.51), while users in the situation of F-C scanned quicker than users in the situation of F-M (43.14 > 32.89).

In the post-switch search, Memory motivation users had more fixations than Complement motivation users (P-M = 0.27 > P-C = 0.25 and F-M = 0.22 > F-C = 0.21). Fixation duration shows a similar trend between users of Memory and Complement motivations (P-M = 0.26 > P-C = 0.25 and F-M = 0.22 > F-C = 0.21). Users in the situation of F-M had a considerable saccadic amplitude, compared with users in the situation of F-C (167.11 > 100.16). As for the scan speed, Memory motivation users scanned more quickly than Complement motivation users (P-M = 34.11 > P-C = 28.82 and F-M = 31.62 > F-C = 25.37).

A further analysis of eye movements over the whole cross-device search shows similar distributions of gaze behavior under different motivations (see Figure 5.17). The two-way ANOVA test confirms there is neither the main effect nor an interaction effect of motivation on gaze behavior (see Table 5.23). Although the screen size of different devices might have an impact on the user's eye movement, the device condition was deemed to be a black box in the current study. We calculated the measures based on the whole search process, ignoring the impact of the device and focusing on the impact of motivation. The findings about eye movement in the current study imply the effect of motivation on gaze during cross-device searching is not significant.

5.7 Effect Size on Observable Cross-device Search Behavior

By the two-way ANOVA analysis, the main effects of either controlled motivation or autonomous motivation on specific features of cross-device search behavior were found. To gain a deep understanding of the effect, a T-test was

100 Cross-device Search Behaviors

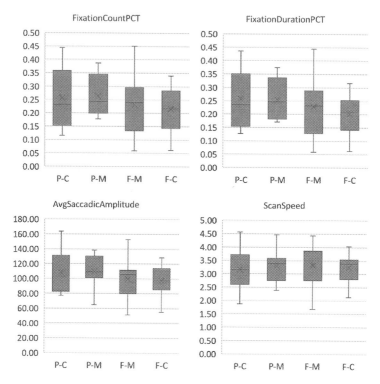

FIGURE 5.17 Eye movements over the whole search (Note: P-C refers to Planned-Complement, P-M refers to Planned-Memory, F-C refers to Forced-Complement, F-M refers to Forced-Memory. The line links the minimum and the maximum. The cross indicates the average.)

TABLE 5.23 Results of two-way ANOVA on eye movements

	\multicolumn{6}{c}{Main effect}	\multicolumn{3}{c}{Interaction effect}
	\multicolumn{3}{c}{Controlled (Planned vs. Forced)}	\multicolumn{3}{c}{Autonomous (Complement vs. Memory)}	\multicolumn{3}{c}{Controlled★ Autonomous}
	df	F	p	df	F	p	df	F	p
FixationCountPCT	1	2.134	0.15	1	0.209	0.649	1	0.032	0.859
FixationDurationPCT	1	3.177	0.08	1	0.232	0.632	1	0.449	0.506
AvgSaccadicAmplitude	1	2.723	0.105	1	0.044	0.835	1	0.002	0.969
ScanSpeed	1	0.112	0.74	1	0.395	0.532	1	0.016	0.901

★p < 0.05, ★★p < 0.01

Cross-device Search Behaviors 101

TABLE 5.24 Effect size of controlled motivation on cross-device search behavior

Measure	Controlled Motivation (Mean ± SD)		t□	p□	Cohen's d
	Planned (n = 26)	Forced (n = 33)			
MaxSERPdepth	1.88 ± 0.86	1.38 ± 0.49	2.676	0.011★	0.746
DownFreq_C	4.58 ± 3.56	2.21 ± 2.37	2.918	0.006★★	0.802
DownLeftFreq_C	13.04 ± 8.54	8.58 ± 5.28	2.335	0.025★	0.646
UpFreq_C	5.00 ± 3.42	3.13 ± 2.54	2.397	0.020★	0.633
UpLeftFreq_C	13.68 ± 6.34	10.24 ± 5.57	2.194	0.032★	0.582
Replacement	0.73 ± 1.04	0.10 ± 0.31	2.956	0.006★★	0.837

★p < 0.05, ★★p < 0.01b

conducted to examine the effect size of motivation on a certain behavioral feature. Table 5.24 shows the results of the T-test on behaviors that were mainly influenced by the controlled motivation. Planned and Forced motivations have a significant impact on clicking, MTI, and query reformulation during the cross-device search. Compared with Forced motivation users, the Planned motivation user would click deeper SERPs, move mouse cursors in directions of down, down-left, up, and up-left, and replace queries with words of partially overlapping meanings. The controlled motivation was found to have a large size of effect on replacement and DownFreq_C (Cohen's d > 0.8). Moreover, there was a medium-sized effect of controlled motivation on MaxSERPdepth, DownLeftFreq_C, UpFreq_C, and UpLeftFreq_C (Cohen's d > 0.5). We can conclude the controlled motivation strongly influences users' behaviors of query constructing and SERP viewing. The effect of controlled motivation on paging and cursor movement is relatively weak.

Table 5.25 displays the results of the T-test on features mainly affected by autonomous motivation. The autonomous motivation was revealed to significantly affect query similarity, click depth, cursor movements, and actions of swiping to the left. When users searched to recall during the cross-device

TABLE 5.25 Effect size of autonomous motivation on cross-device search behavior

Measure	Autonomous Motivation (Mean ± SD)		t□	p□	Cohen's d
	Complement (n = 31)	Memory (n = 28)			
JaccardSimilarity	0.20 ± 0.09	0.27 ± 0.14	−2.264	0.028★	0.601
AveClickDepth	4.46 ± 0.85	3.93 ± 0.76	2.508	0.015★	0.66
DownSpeed_M	367.94 ± 144.46	471.35 ± 169.29	−2.467	0.017★	0.661
LeftSpeed_M	26.47 ± 44.04	3.09 ± 9.59	2.823	0.008★★	0.692
DownLeftSpeed_C	171.81 ± 58.26	245.44 ± 144.30	−2.515	0.017★	0.678

★p < 0.05, ★★p < 0.01

search, they would issue queries with similar meanings, click results that ranked at the top, quickly swipe down, slowly swipe left, and quickly move the cursor down-left. The effect of autonomous motivation on these behaviors is at a medium level (Cohen's d > 0.5). It seems the speed of MTI to the left is influenced by autonomous motivation at the highest level (Cohen's d = 0.692), followed by DownLeftSpeed_C, DownSpeed_M, AveClickDepth, and JaccardSimilarity in sequence.

5.8 Cognition of Cross-device Search

5.8.1 Subjective Evaluation of Cross-device Search

Users were required to evaluate their subjective feelings about the upcoming search, and evaluate it again after finishing the search. The results of the subjective evaluation before and after searching are compared in Figure 5.18. In the pre-search survey, users assessed familiarity, clarity, difficulty, and confidence about the upcoming search. It should be noted that Planned motivation users were not notified of the cross-device search when doing the evaluation. In this case, the evaluation of all users was under the same condition, where the user had not interfered with any designed motivation. It can be seen that all users were confident with the upcoming search, which indicates they expected that they would perform well. In the post-search survey, users assessed familiarity, clarity, difficulty, and satisfaction based on the experience of cross-device searching under different motivational situations. It was observed that users in the situation of F-M perceived the highest satisfaction, while users in the situation of P-C had the lowest satisfaction. The evaluation of satisfaction indicated the search performance the users actually felt. Users would have a good performance of cross-device searching when aiming to recall by search or engaging in a cross-device search without preparation. Evaluations of familiarity, clarity, and difficulty were repeated after the search. Comparing the change between pre- and post-search offers a glimpse of the effect of motivation on users' subjective feelings about

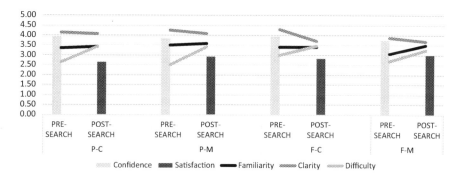

FIGURE 5.18 Comparison of subjective evaluation between pre-search and post-search

Cross-device Search Behaviors **103**

TABLE 5.26 Results of paired samples T-test on subjective evaluation

Motivation	Measure	t□	p□	Cohen's d
P-C	Familiarity	0.211	0.836	0.056
	Clarity	−0.221	0.828	0.059
	Difficulty	3.294	0.006**	0.88
P-M	Familiarity	0.266	0.795	0.077
	Clarity	−0.561	0.586	0.162
	Difficulty	3.188	0.009**	0.92
F-C	Familiarity	0	1	0
	Clarity	−2.582	0.020*	0.626
	Difficulty	1.646	0.119	0.399
F-M	Familiarity	2.15	0.048*	0.538
	Clarity	−0.764	0.456	0.191
	Difficulty	2.058	0.057	0.514

*p < 0.05, **p < 0.01

cross-device searching. The trend of changes is similar among different motivations, where the evaluation of clarity dropped, and the evaluation of familiarity and difficulty rose. However, the degree of changes differs among different motivations, which demonstrates the effect of motivation on user cognition. A paired-samples T-test was carried out to test the significance of the effect (see Table 5.26), and shows that the situations of P-C ($p = 0.006 < 0.01$) and P-M ($p = 0.009 < 0.01$) have a significant impact on the users' perceived difficulty about the cross-device search. The effect of P-M is more outstanding than that of P-C (Cohen's d $= 0.88 < 0.92$). Users' clarity significantly decreases in the situation of F-C ($p = 0.020 < 0.05$). In addition, users' familiarity with the search significantly increases in the situation of F-M ($p = 0.048 < 0.05$).

5.8.2 Search Strategies of Cross-device Search

We conducted a content analysis of the interview transcripts to reveal users' search strategies during cross-device searches under different motivations. We open-coded the transcripts to establish properties of the search strategy and compared differences between motivations. In the experiment, we asked users about their thoughts and feelings when they were faced with different situations. Q1 was asked of all users when they read the search task and had not yet started to search. In other words, users discussed their thoughts and feelings about the upcoming search without any effect of the designed motivations. Q2 was asked when the user was aware of the Planned or Forced motivation and had not begun or continued the search. This reveals the impact of these motivations that the user expected to have. The distinction between the Planned and Forced motivations is whether the interruption of switching a device is expected. Q6 asked about the user's thoughts and feelings on the interruption, either expected or not, when the search ended. Q6 reveals what impact of the Planned or Forced motivation the user perceived. The difference between the Planned and Forced motivations was compared on the basis of Q2 and Q6. Similarly, Q3 was asked when the user was aware of the Memory or Complement motivation and did not continue the search. The answers indicated what impact of the Memory or Complement motivation the user expected to have on the subsequent searching. Q7 was asked when the search ended, which collected the user's perception of the influence of motivation. The difference between the Memory and Complement motivations could be seen through Q3 and Q7. Q4 and Q5 were designed as a supplement, asking users' thoughts about and understanding of cross-device searching.

When receiving the description of the search task, most users described a step-by-step search strategy. They described their search plan in the form of "at first, I will..., and then..." User No. 30 said, "the first thing is to search for the school rankings, then go to the official websites of these schools to see information about admission." The reason for adopting this step-by-step search strategy is the multifaceted characteristics of the search task. In controlled experiments, users will commonly search information in sequence following the description of the task. As user No. 18 said, "(I will) just follow the task, one by one, to search." A few users utilized another type of search strategy, which listed several alternative solutions. For example, user No. 58 prepared three methods to search for the task, saying, "I think the last one is probably the most reliable of these three methods." According to users' thoughts about the upcoming search, several properties are noteworthy, the first being prior knowledge. When formulating a search plan, users would make reference to past experiences of a similar topic. Users tended to find information from sources that they were acquainted with. For example, user No. 54 said, "I'm going to look at information from Yanzhao website, because I have visited this site before." Another mentioned property is information source. Users cared a great deal about the officialness and authority of information sources where they would adopt information when they developed search strategies. "(Information will be) available on the particular law school's website," said user No. 29. Another mentioned property is the evaluation of difficulty. Many users estimated the difficulty of a search before beginning. They directly stated how difficult they felt it would be, or they indirectly evaluated the difficulty by saying, as user No. 77 did, "(the task) is close to my life." Finally, yet another mentioned property is the anticipation of obstacles. Users were observed to anticipate problems that might occur during the search and think ahead for solutions. For example, user No. 64 declared that she would consult training institution websites if she could not find information from official sites. These properties demonstrate what concerns users when they are developing search strategies.

Facing the different motivations of Planned and Forced, different search plans for the upcoming search were witnessed among some users. For Forced motivation users, their search was suddenly interrupted and they were unexpectedly told to change devices. Although they were surprised by the device transition, most users continued the search as initially planned, since they thought the search system provided the same results no matter what device was used. A few users worried it would take time to get used to the new device, which might slow down their search efficiency (e.g., user No. 19). However, this worry did not change the method of searching. For Planned motivation users, things were different. Some users shared the opinion that the device has no impact on search results. Thus, they kept their original search strategy that they mapped out when reading the task. Other users changed their search strategy by assigning search content to different devices. It was thought by some users that the inconvenience of mobile phones would lead to poor search performance. In this case, they preferred to search more on desktop and utilize mobile search as a supplement. After completing the search, not all users acknowledged the effect of Planned and Forced motivations on their search. For those who perceived the effect, the effect was more on emotions rather than search strategies. For instance, Planned motivation user No. 04 felt confident with the information she found.

Speaking of the effect of Memory and Complement motivations on search strategies, the difference was perceived more strongly when users finished the search. Memory motivation users became more confident with result selection. User No. 03 stated he had a more specific purpose in the post-switch search and selected results more accurately. Searching on different devices helps the user be sure about what information is actually wanted. Finding the same information on a different device confirms the user obtained the correct information. For Complement motivation users, it was agreed the experience of pre-switch searching helped optimize the post-switch search. Search experience on the anterior device improved the user's strategy of constructing queries. Users learned how to modify the query and could obtain relevant results based on their experiences of failure in the pre-switch search. Complement motivation user No. 56 described her pre-switch search as wide, and the post-switch search became focused.

5.9 Summary

Based on the four main motivations obtained in Chapter 3, i.e., planned cross-device search (Planned), forced to interrupt the search (Forced), helping memory (Memory), and complementing existing search results (Complement), this chapter further explores cross-device search behavior under different motivations. The four motivations are classified either as controlled (i.e., planned vs. forced) or autonomous (i.e., memory vs. complement) motivations according to the classic psychological theory, self-determination theory (SDT).

This chapter conducts a controlled experiment and analyzes the effects of motivation on cross-device search behavior. The self-developed CAFE search system, Tobii Pro X3-120 Eye Tracker, and Tobii Pro Mobile Device Stand were used in the experiment, supplemented by questionnaires and interviews, to collect users' behavioral data in aspects of queries, clicks, desktop cursor movements, mobile touch interactions, eye movements, and cognition in the process of cross-device

106 Cross-device Search Behaviors

TABLE 5.27 Summary of the effects of motivation on cross-device search behaviors

Motivation dimension (Type)	Search behavior	Measures
Controlled Motivation (planned vs. forced)	Query	Replacement
	Click	MaxSERPdepth
	MTI	DownFreq_C、DownLeftFreq_C、UpFreq_C、UpLeftFreq_C
	Cognition	Familiarity, clarity, difficulty
Autonomous Motivation (memory vs. complement)	Query	JaccardSimilarity
	Click	AveClickDepth
	Cursor Movement	DownLeftSpeed_C
	MTI	DownSpeed_M、LeftSpeed_M
	Cognition	Familiarity, clarity, difficulty

searching. The characteristics of different types of cross-device search behaviors under different motivations are analyzed by combining quantitative and qualitative analysis methods. According to the relevant research on information search behavior, this chapter selects a variety of behavioral measures and compares the differences of search behavior under different motivations from three levels: preswitch search, post-switch search, and over the entire cross-device search process.

Then, the effects of controlled and autonomous motivation on search behavior were tested by the statistical analysis method. Results are summarized in Table 5.27. It was found that controlled motivation had significant effects on click behavior, touch interaction and query reformulation; autonomous motivation had significant effects on query similarity, click depth, cursor movement and swiping to the left; different motivations had significant effects on users' perceived familiarity, difficulty and clarity. According to the interviews, with controlled motivation, a portion of users showed differences in search strategy for the upcoming search; with autonomous motivation, users perceived stronger differences in search strategy when the search was completed.

References

Agichtein, E., White, R. W., Dumais, S. T., & Bennet, P. N. (2012). Search, interrupted: Understanding and predicting search task continuation. In *Proceedings of the 35th International ACM Sigir Conference on Research and Development in Information Retrieval* (pp. 315–324). doi:10.1145/2348283.2348328

Alhenshiri, A., Walters, C., Shepherd, M., & Duffy, J. (2012). Investigating web information gathering tasks. *Proceedings of the ASIST Annual Meeting, 49*(1), 109–118. doi:10.1002/meet.14504901281

Baeza-Yates, R., Calderón-Benavides, L., & González-Caro, C. (2006). The intention behind web queries: Processing and information retrieval. SPIRE 2006. *Lecture Notes in Computer Science, 4209*, 98–109. doi:10.1007/11880561_9

Belkin, N. J. (1980). Anomalous states of knowledge as a basis for information retrieval. *Canadian Journal of Information Science, 5*(1), 133–143.

Bhattacharya, N., & Gwizdka, J. (2018). Relating eye-tracking measures with changes in knowledge on search I tasks. In *Proceedings of the 2018 ACM Symposium on Eye Tracking Research & Applications* (pp. 1–5). doi:10.1145/3204493.3204579

Broder, A. (2002). A taxonomy of web search. *ACM SIGIR Forum, 36*(2), 3–10. doi:10.1145/792550.792552

Burkhardt, D., Pattan, S., Nazemi, K., & Kuijper, A. (2017). Search intention analysis for task- and user-centered visualization in big data applications. *Procedia Computer Science, 104,* 539–547. doi:10.1016/j.procs.2017.01.170.

Buscher, G., Dumais, S. T., & Cutrell, E. (2010). The good, the bad, and the random: An eye-tracking study of ad quality in web search. In *Proceedings of the 33rd International ACM SIGIR Conference on Research and Development in Information Retrieval* (pp. 42–49). doi:10.1145/1835449.1835459

Case, D. O. (2012). *Looking for information: A survey of research on information seeking, needs and behavior.* Bingley: Emerald Group Publishing.

Cecchinato, M. E., Sellen, A., Shokouhi, M., & Smyth, G. (2016). Finding email in a multi-account, multi-device world. In *ACM CHI Conference on Human Factors in Computing Systems, USA* (pp. 1200–1210). doi:10.1145/2858036.2858473

Cutrell, E., & Guan, Z. (2007). What are you looking for? An eye-tracking study of information usage in web search. In *Proceedings of the SIGCHI Conference on Human Factors in Computing Systems* (pp. 407–416). doi:10.1145/1240624.1240690

Dearman, D., & Pierce, J. S. (2008). "It's on my other computer!": Computing with multiple devices. In *ACM SIGIR Conference on Human Factors in Computing Systems, Italy* (pp. 767–776) doi:10.1145/1357054.1357177

Deci, E. L., & Ryan, R. M. (1985). *Intrinsic motivation and self-determination in human motivation.* New York: Plenum Press.

Deci, E. L., & Ryan, R. M. (2008). Self-determination theory: A macrotheory of human motivation, development, and health. *Canadian Psychology/Psychologie Canadienne, 49,* 182–185. doi:10.1037/a0012801

Dervin, B. (1998). Sense-making theory and practice: An overview of user interests in knowledge seeking and use. *Journal of Knowledge Management, 2*(2), 36–46. doi:10.1108/13673279810249369

Dubnjakovic, A. (2017). Information seeking motivation scale development: A self-determination perspective. *Journal of Documentation, 73*(5), 1034–1052. doi:10.1108/JD-03-2017-0032

Dubnjakovic, A. (2018). Antecedents and consequences of autonomous information seeking motivation. *Library & Information Science Research, 40*(1), 9–17. doi:10.1016/j.lisr.2018.03.003.

Ellison, N. B., Triệu, P., Schoenebeck, S., Brewer, R., & Israni, A. (2020). Why we don't click: Interrogating the relationship between viewing and clicking in social media contexts by exploring the "Non-Click". *Journal of Computer-Mediated Communication, 25*(6), 402–426. doi:10.1093/jcmc/zmaa013

Fidel, R. (1985). Moves in online searching. *Online Review, 9*(1), 61–74.

Geronimo, L. D., Husmann, M., & Norrie, M. C. (2016, June). Surveying personal device ecosystems with cross-device applications in mind. In *ACM International Symposium on Pervasive Displays, Finland* (pp. 220–227) doi:10.1145/2914920.2915028

Ginsca, A. L., Popescu, A., & Lupu, M. (2015). Credibility in information retrieval. *Foundations and Trends® in Information Retrieval, 9*(5), 355–475. doi:10.1561/1500000046

Granka, L. A., Joachims, T., & Gay, G. (2004). Eye-tracking analysis of user behavior in WWW search. In *Proceedings of the 27th Annual International ACM SIGIR Conference on Research and Development in Information Retrieval* (pp. 478–479). doi:10.1145/1008992.1009079

Guo, Q., & Agichtein, E. (2010). Ready to buy or just browsing?: detecting web searcher goals from interaction data. In *Proceedings of the International ACM SIGIR Conference on Research and Development in Information Retrieval* (pp. 130–137).

Guo, Q., Jin, H., Lagun, D., Yuan, S., & Agichtein, E. (2013). Mining touch interaction data on mobile devices to predict web search result relevance. In *Proceedings of the 36th International ACM SIGIR Conference on Research and Development in Information Retrieval* (pp. 153–162). doi:10.1145/2484028.2484100

Guo, Q., Yuan, S., & Agichtein, E. (2011). Detecting success in mobile search from interaction. In *Proceedings of the 34th International ACM SIGIR Conference on Research and Development in Information Retrieval* (pp. 1229–1230). doi:10.1145/2009916.2010133

Gwizdka, J., & Bilal, D. (2017). Analysis of children's queries and click behavior on ranked results and their thought processes in Google search. In *Proceedings of the 2017 Conference on Conference Human Information Interaction and Retrieval* (pp. 377–380). doi:10.1145/3020165.3022157

Han, S., He, D., & Chi, Y. (2017). Understanding and modeling behavior patterns in cross-device web search. In *Proceedings of the Association for Information Science and Technology* (pp. 150–158). doi:10.1002/pra2.2017.14505401017

Han, S., He, D., Yue, Z., & Brusilovsky, P. (2015). Supporting cross-device web search with social navigation-based mobile touch interactions. In *Proceedings of the International Conference on User Modeling*, Adaptation and Personalization (pp. 143–155). doi:10.1007/978-3-319-20267-9_12

Han, S., Yue, Z., & He, D. (2015). Understanding and supporting cross-device web search for exploratory tasks with mobile touch interactions. *ACM Transactions on Information Systems, 33*(4), 1–34. doi:10.1145/2738036

Huang, J., White, R. W., & Buscher, G. (2012). User see, user point: Gaze and cursor alignment in web search. In *Proceedings of the SIGCHI Conference on Human Factors in Computing Systems* (pp. 1341–1350). doi:10.1145/2207676.2208591

Huang, J., White, R. W., & Dumais, S. (2011). No clicks, no problem: Using cursor movements to understand and improve search. In *Proceedings of the SIGCHI Conference on Human Factors in Computing Systems* (pp. 1225–1234). doi:10.1145/1978942.1979125

Jain, V., & Varma, M. (2011). Learning to re-rank: Query-dependent image re-ranking using click data. In *Proceedings of the 20th International Conference on World Wide Web* (pp. 277–286). doi:10.1145/1963405.1963447

Jansen, B. J., Booth, D. L., & Spink, A. (2009). Patterns of query reformulation during Web searching. *Journal of the American Society for Information Science and Technology, 60*(7), 1358–1371. doi:10.1002/asi.21071

Kane, S. K., Karlson, A. K., Meyers, B. R., Johns, P., Jacobs, A., & Smith, G. (2009). Exploring cross-device web use on PCs and mobile devices. In *IFIP TC 13 International Conference on Human-Computer Interaction, Sweden* (pp. 722–735). doi:10.1007/978-3-642-03655-2_79

Kellar, M., Watters, C., & Shepherd, M. (2007). A field study characterizing Web-based information-seeking tasks. *Journal of the American Society for Information Science and Technology, 58*(7), 999–1018. doi:10.1002/asi.20590

Kelly, D., Arguello, J., Edwards, A., & Wu, W. (2015). Development and evaluation of search tasks for IIR experiments using a cognitive complexity framework. In *Proceedings of the 2015 International Conference on The Theory of Information Retrieval (ICTIR '15)* (pp. 101–110). doi:10.1145/2808194.2809465

Kim, J., Thomas, P., Sankaranarayana, R., Gedeon, T., & Yoon, H. (2017). What snippet size is needed in mobile web search? In *Proceedings of the 2017 Conference on Conference Human Information Interaction and Retrieval* (pp. 97–106). doi:10.1145/3020165.3020173

Kim, J., Thomas, P., Sankaranarayana, R., Gedeon, T., & Yoon, H. J. (2015). Eye-tracking analysis of user behavior and performance in web search on large and small screens. *Journal of the Association for Information Science and Technology, 66*(3), 526–544. doi:10.1002/asi.23187

Kim, J., Thomas, P., Sankaranarayana, R., Gedeon, T., & Yoon, H. J. (2016). Understanding eye movements on mobile devices for better presentation of search results. *Journal of the Association for Information Science and Technology, 67*(11), 2607–2619. doi:10.1002/asi.23628

Kim, S., Kini, N., Koh, E., Koh, E., & Getoor, L. (2017, April). Probabilistic visitor stitching on cross-device web logs. In *International Conference on World Wide Web*, Australia (pp. 1581–1589) doi:10.1145/3038912.3052711

Kotov, A., Bennett, P. N., White, R. W., Dumais, S. T., & Teevan, J. (2011). Modeling and analysis of cross-session search tasks. In *Proceedings of the International ACM SIGIR Conference on Research and Development in Information Retrieval* (pp. 5–14). doi:10.1145/2009916.2009922

Kuhlthau, C. C. (1991). Inside the search process: Information seeking from the user's perspective. *Journal of the American Society for Information Science, 42*(5), 361–371. doi:10.1002/(SICI)1097-4571(199106)42:5<361::AID-ASI6>3.0.CO;2-%23

Li, R., Li, L., Wu, X., Zhou, Y., & Wang, W. (2019). Click feedback-aware query recommendation using adversarial examples. In *The World Wide Web Conference* (pp. 2978–2984). doi:10.1145/3308558.3313412

Li, Y., Capra, R., & Zhang, Y. (2020). Everyday cross-session search: How and why do people search across multiple sessions? In *Proceedings of the 2020 Conference on Human Information Interaction and Retrieval* (pp. 163–172). doi:10.1145/3343413.3377970

Lin, S. J. (2005). Internetworking of factors affecting successive searches over multiple episodes. *Journal of the American Society for Information Science and Technology, 56*(4), 416–436. doi:10.1002/asi.20128

Lin, S. J., & Belkin, N. J. (2000). Modeling multiple information seeking episodes. In *Proceedings of the 63rd Annual Meeting of the American Society for Information Science* (pp. 133–147).

Lin, S. J., & Belkin, N. J. (2005). Validation of a model of information seeking over multiple search sessions. *Journal of the American Society for Information Science and Technology, 56*(4), 393–415. doi:10.1002/asi.20127

Lin, S. J. & Xie, I. (2013). Behavioral changes in transmuting multisession successive searches over the web. *Journal of the American Society for Information Science and Technology, 64*, 1259–1283. doi:10.1002/asi.22839

Liu, C., Gwizdka, J., Liu, J., Xu, T., & Belkin, N. J. (2010). Analysis and evaluation of query reformulations in different task types. *Proceedings of the American Society for Information Science and Technology, 47*(1), 1–9.

Liu, J., & Belkin, N. J. (2015). Personalizing information retrieval for multi-session tasks: Examining the roles of task stage, task type, and topic knowledge on the interpretation of dwell time as an indicator of document usefulness. *Journal of The Association for Information Science and Technology, 66*(1), 58–81. doi:10.1002/asi.23160

Liu, J., Belkin, N. J., Zhang, X., & Yuan, X. (2013). Examining users' knowledge change in the task completion process. *Information Processing and Management, 49*(2013), 1058–1074. doi:10.1016/j.ipm.2012.08.006

Liu, J., Mitsui, M., Belkin, N. J., & Shah, C. (2019). Task, information seeking intentions, and user behavior: Toward a multi-level understanding of web search. In *Proceedings of the 2019 Conference on Human Information Interaction and Retrieval (CHIIR '19)* (pp. 123–132). doi:10.1145/3295750.3298922

MacKay, B., & Watters, C. (2012). An examination of multisession web tasks. *Journal of the American Society for Information Science and Technology, 63*(6), 1183–1197. doi:10.1002/asi.22610

Marshall, C., & Lindley, S. (2014). Searching for myself: Motivations and strategies for self-search. In *Conference on Human Factors in Computing Systems-Proceedings* (pp. 3675–3684). doi:10.1145/2556288.2557356.

Martín-Albo, D., Leiva, L. A., Huang, J., & Plamondon, R. (2016). Strokes of insight: User intent detection and kinematic compression of mouse cursor trails, *Information Processing & Management, 52*(6), 989–1003. doi:10.1016/j.ipm.2016.04.005.

Montañez, G. D., White, R. W., & Huang, X. (2014, November). Cross-device search. In *ACM International Conference on Conference on Information & Knowledge Management*, China (pp. 1669–1678). doi:10.1145/2661829.2661910

Morris, D., Morris, M. R., & Venolia, G. (2008). Search Bar: A search-centric web history for task resumption and information re-finding. In *Conference on Human Factors in Computing Systems Proceedings* (pp. 1207–1216). doi:10.1145/1357054.1357242

Rha, E. Y., Shi, W., & Belkin, N. J. (2017). An exploration of reasons for query reformulations. In *Proceedings of the Association for Information Science and Technology* (pp. 337–346.) doi:10.1002/pra2.2017.14505401037

Rieh, S. Y., & Xie, H. (2006). Analysis of multiple query reformulations on the web: The interactive information retrieval context. *Information Processing & Management, 42*(3), 751–768. doi:10.1016/j.ipm.2005.05.005

Ryan, R. M., & Deci, E. L. (2000). Intrinsic and extrinsic motivations: Classic definitions and new directions. *Contemporary Educational Psychology, 25*, 54–67. doi:10.1006/ceps.1999.1020

Ryan, R. M., & Deci, E. L. (2020). Intrinsic and extrinsic motivation from a self-determination theory perspective: Definitions, theory, practices, and future directions, *Contemporary Educational Psychology, 61*, 101860. doi:10.1016/j.cedpsych.2020.101860.

Santos, P. A., Madeira, R. N., & Correia, N. (2018, November). Designing a framework to support the development of smart cross-device applications. In *The 17th International Conference on Mobile and Ubiquitous Multimedia*, Egypt (pp. 367–374). doi:10.1145/3282894.3289727

Savolainen, R. (2008). Autonomous, controlled and half-hearted. Unemployed people's motivations to seek information about jobs. *Information Research, 13*(1), 362.

Savolainen, R. (2018). Self-determination and expectancy-value: Comparison of cognitive psychological approaches to motivators for information seeking about job opportunities. *Aslib Journal of Information Management, 70*(1), 123–140. doi:10.1108/AJIM-10-2017-0242

Sculley, D., Malkin, R. G., Basu, S., & Bayardo, R. J. (2009). Predicting bounce rates in sponsored search advertisements. In *Proceedings of the ACM SIGKDD International Conference on Knowledge Discovery and Data Mining* (pp. 1325–1334).

Sellen, A. J., Murphy, R., & Shaw, K. L. (2002). How knowledge workers use the web. In *Proceedings of the SIGCHI Conference on Human Factors in Computing Systems (CHI'02)* (pp. 227–234). doi:10.1145/503376.503418

Sohn, T., Battestini, A., Horii, H., Bales, E., Setlur, V., & Mori, K. (2010, November). Supporting unplanned activities through cross-device interaction. In *International Conference on Automotive User Interfaces & Interactive Vehicular Applications*, Pennsylvania (pp. 146–147) doi:10.1145/1969773.1969800

Sohn, T., Mori, K., & Setlur, V. (2010, April). Enabling cross-device interaction with web history. In *CHI'10 Extended Abstracts on Human Factors in Computing Systems*, Georgia (pp. 3883–3888) doi:10.1145/1753846.1754073

Soleymani, M., Riegler, M., & Halvorsen, P. (2017). Multimodal analysis of image search intent: Intent recognition in image search from user behavior and visual content. In *Proceedings of the 2017 ACM on International Conference on Multimedia Retrieval (ICMR '17)* (pp. 251–259). doi:10.1145/3078971.3078995

Spink, A. (1996). Multiple search sessions model of end-user behavior: An exploratory study. *Journal of the Association for Information Science & Technology, 47,* 603–609. doi:10.1002/(SICI)1097-4571(199608)47:8<603::AID-ASI4>3.0.CO;2-X

Spink, A., Bateman, J., & Griesdorf, H. (1998). Successive searching behavior during information retrieval (IR): Development of a new line of research. In *Proceedings of the 26th Annual Meeting of the Canadian Association for Information Science* (pp. 401–415).

Spink, A., Griesdorf, H., & Bateman, J. (1999). A study of mediated successive searching during information seeking. *Journal of Information Science, 25*(6), 477–487. doi:10.1177/016555159902500604

Spink, A., Wilson, T., Ellis, D., & Ford, N. (1998). Modeling users' successive searches in digital environments: A National Science Foundation/British Library Funded Study. *D-Lib Magazine, 4*(4).

Spink, A., Wilson, T., Ford, N., Foster, A., & Ellis, D. (2002). Information seeking and mediated searching study. Part 3. Successive searching. *Journal of the Association for Information Science & Technology, 53,* 716–727. doi:10.1002/asi.10083

Strohmeier, P. (2015, November). Display pointers: Seamless cross-device interactions. In *International Conference on Advances in Computer Entertainment Technology,* Malaysia (pp. 1–8). doi:10.1145/2832932.2832958

Tanielian, U., Tousch, A. M., & Vasile, F. (2018, April). Siamese cookie embedding networks for cross-device user matching. In *The Web Conference,* France (pp. 85–86). doi:10.1145/3184558.3186941

Taylor, R. S. (1968). Question-negotiation and information seeking in libraries. *College and Research Libraries, 29,* 178–194. doi:10.5860/crl_29_03_178.

Tran, J. J., Trewin, S., Swart, C., John, B. E., & Thomas, J. C. (2013). Exploring pinch and spread gestures on mobile devices. In *Proceedings of the 15th International Conference on Human-Computer Interaction with Mobile Devices and Services* (pp. 151–160). doi:10.1145/2493190.2493221

Tso, G. K. F., Yau, K. K. W., & Cheung, M. S. M. (2010). Latent constructs determining Internet job search behaviors: Motivation, opportunity and job change intention. *Computers in Human Behavior, 26*(2), 122–131. doi:10.1016/j.chb.2009.10.016.

Turner, J. (2013). Cross-device eye-based interaction. In *Proceedings of the Adjunct Publication of the 26th Annual ACM Symposium on User Interface Software and Technology* (pp. 37–40). doi:10.1145/2508468.2508471

Tyler, S. K., Wang, J., & Zhang, Y. (2010). Utilizing re-finding for personalized information retrieval. In *Proceedings of the ACM International Conference on Information and Knowledge Management* (pp. 1469–1472). doi:10.1145/1871437.1871649

Tyler, S. K., & Zhang, Y. (2012). Multi-session re-search: In pursuit of repetition and diversification. In *Proceedings of the 21st ACM International Conference on Information and Knowledge Management* (pp. 2055–2059). do:10.1145/2396761.2398571

Wang, H., Song, Y., Chang, M. W., & Chu W. (2013). Learning to extract cross-session search tasks. In *Proceedings of the 22nd International Conference on World Wide Web* (pp. 1353–1364). doi:10.1145/2488388.2488507

Wang, Y., Huang, X., & White, R. W. (2013, February). Characterizing and supporting cross-device search tasks. In *ACM International Conference on Web Search & Data Mining,* Italy (pp. 707–716). 10.1145/2433396.2433484

White, R. W., & Horvitz, E. (2014). From health search to healthcare: Explorations of intention and utilization via query logs and user surveys. *Journal of the American Medical Informatics Association, 21*(1), 49–55. doi:10.1136/amiajnl-2012-001473.

Wu, D., & Bi, R. (2017), Impact of device on search pattern transitions: A comparative study based on large-scale library OPAC log data. *The Electronic Library, 35*(4), 650–666. doi:10.1108/EL-10-2016-0239

Wu, D., Dong, J., & Liu, C. (2019). Exploratory study of cross-device search tasks. *Information Processing & Management, 56*(6), 102073. doi:10.1016/j.ipm.2019.102073

Wu, D, Dong, J, Tang, Y., & Capra, R. (2020). Understanding task preparation and resumption behaviors in cross-device search. *Journal of the Association for Information Science and Technology, 71*, 887–901. doi:10.1002/asi.24307

Wu, D., Liang, S., & Bi, R. (2018). Characterizing queries in cross-device OPAC search: A large-scale log study. *Library Hi Tech, 36*(3), 482–497. doi:10.1108/LHT-06-2017-0130

Wu, D., & Yuan, F. (2018). Exploring dynamic change of users' cross-device search performance. In *Proceedings of the Association for Information Science and Technology* (pp. 931–932). doi:10.1002/pra2.2018.14505501181

Yaneva, V., Ha, L. A., Eraslan, S., Yesilada, Y., & Mitkov, R. (2018). Detecting autism based on eye-tracking data from web searching tasks. In *Proceedings of the Internet of Accessible Things* (pp. 1–10). doi:10.1145/3192714.3192819

Youngmann, B., & Yom-Tov, E. (2018). Anxiety and information seeking: Evidence from large-scale mouse tracking. In *Proceedings of the 2018 World Wide Web Conference* (pp. 753–762). doi:10.1145/3178876.3186156

Yue, Z., Han, S., & He, D. (2013). An investigation of the query behavior in task-based collaborative exploratory web search. In *Proceedings of the 76th ASIS & T Annual Meeting: Beyond the Cloud: Rethinking Information Boundaries (ASIST '13)* (pp. 1–10).

Zhang, Y., Chen, W., Wang, D., & Yang, Q. (2011). User-click modeling for understanding and predicting search-behavior. In *Proceedings of the 17th ACM SIGKDD International Conference on Knowledge Discovery and Data Mining* (pp. 1388–1396). doi:10.1145/2020408.2020613

6

CROSS-DEVICE SEARCH BEHAVIOR MODELING

6.1 Review of Cross-device Search-Related Behavior Modeling

6.1.1 The approach of Search Behavior Modeling

Search behavior modeling is a classic method of understanding a specific information-seeking behavior. Traditional search behavior modeling relies on qualitative approaches, for example, Ellis's model of information-searching strategies (Ellis, 1989), Kuhlthau's Information Search Process (Kuhlthau, 1993), and Wilson's problem-solving model (Wilson, 1997). Structural or semi-structural interviews were conducted to collect data. In order to maximize the credibility of data collection and analysis, studies usually follow a rigorous procedure, such as the criteria used by Lincoln and Guba (1985). A typical case can be seen in the development of the nonlinear model of information-seeking behavior (Foster, 2004). Triangulation (which applies multiple sources, methods, investigators, or theory to a study) and member checking methods were included in Foster's study in order to increase its credibility. Behavior patterns have been identified by content analysis of interview transcripts (Zach, 2005). Savolainen (2019) modeled information behavior by examining the connections between information seeking and sharing using conceptual analysis. Conceptual analysis is a method that considers the components of a study as classes of objects, events, properties, or relationships (Furner, 2004). Conceptual analysis in practice involves distinguishing terms, analyzing the understandings they refer to, and representing this.

With the development of data collection and data processing techniques, the utilization of quantitative methods in search behavior modeling emerges. The statistical modeling method (e.g., structural equation method) is a popular approach (Kinley, Tjondronegoro, Partridge, & Edwards, 2014). Cao, Zhang, Xu, and Wang (2016) hypothesized a structural regression model of online health

DOI: 10.4324/9780429201677-6

information-seeking behavior based on Wilson's model of information behavior. Data were collected by a large-scale questionnaire investigation, and a maximum likelihood structural equation modeling was performed. With the approach of the big data era, machine learning methods are frequently observed in search behavior modeling (Kim, Craswell, Dumais, Radlinski, & Liu, 2017). Search behavior models developed in this way are useful in prediction and recommendation (Yang, Yan, Yu, Li, & Chiu, 2017). Large-scale search engine logs provide rich data, and diverse behavior features can be involved in modeling.

6.1.2 Cross-session Search Behavior Modeling

The predecessor of cross-session search modeling is regarded as successive searching in the literature. Spink and her colleagues found that most users searched between 1 and 6 sessions through their information-seeking process. Many users interacted with multiple information sources and adapted their search strategies during a long and complex task project (Spink, 1996; Spink, Griesdorf, & Bateman, 1999; Spink, Wilson, Ellis, & Ford, 1998). Encouraged by Spink's study, Lin and Belkin (2000) proposed a conceptual model of cross-session search called "Multiple Information Seeking Episode (MISE)." This model describes the reason for and process of searching for the essentially same information problem across multiple sessions. Wang, Song, Chang, and Chu (2013) developed a semi-supervised model to extract cross-session search tasks from users' search activities. Another exploration of modeling user search behavior that extends over multiple search sessions applied features of individual queries and long-term user search behavior (Kotov, Bennett, White, Dumais, & Teevan, 2011).

6.1.3 Cross-device Search Behavior Modeling

Exploration of modeling cross-device search behavior is limited since cross-device searching is a new topic of interest. Among the few existing studies, to our knowledge, Wang, Huang, and White (2013) took the first step in cross-device search modeling. They conducted a log analysis to characterize cross-device search behavior and predict the resumption of cross-device tasks. Montañez, White, and Huang (2014) were also interested in studying searching across devices and proposed models to predict cross-device search transitions. Han, He, and Chi (2017) used the hidden Markov model (HMM) to model observed cross-device search behaviors in two types of cross-device situations: mobile-to-desktop and desktop-to-desktop. The most recent exploration in this area proposed the method of modeling task preparation and resumption in cross-device searches (Wu, Dong, Tang, & Capra, 2020).

Both qualitative and quantitative methods have been adopted in search behavior modeling. Qualitative modeling is preferred when case studies or interviews are conducted, while quantitative modeling accompanies log analysis. In the current study, Chapter 5 details the rich data of different types of search behavior by logs that was collected; therefore, the machine learning method was applied to develop a cross-device search behavior model. In addition, the current study aims to model cross-device searches under different motivations. The machine learning method can provide the value of model performance, which presents the effective combination of behavior features for identifying different motivations.

6.2 Modeling Cross-device Search Behavior under Different Motivations

6.2.1 Features

Cross-device search is a multidimensional behavior consisting of querying, clicking, cursor moving on desktops, touching on mobile devices, gaze, and cognition. In Chapter 5, we discussed the characteristics of these specific behaviors through corresponding measures. Measures of observable behaviors were adopted as features to model cross-device search behavior, as shown in Table 6.1.

Unlike cross-device search modeling in previous work (Wang, Huang, & White, 2013), we aimed to develop search behavior models under different motivations. The two-way ANOVA analysis shows some behavior measures were significantly affected by either the controlled motivation or the autonomous motivation. These measures were grouped into BASE_C and BASE_A as baseline features for training a cross-device search behavior model under controlled and autonomous motivations. Features related to queries and clicks have been frequently used to model search behavior (Kotov et al., 2011). The QUERY group includes 13 features related to query count, query length, query reformulation, and query semantics, and this shows the advantage of distinguishing search intentions in existing explorations (Burkhardt, Pattan, Nazemi, & Kuijper, 2017; Rha, Mitsui, Belkin, & Shah, 2016; White & Horvitz, 2014). The CLICK group consists of five features related to clicks on SERPs. Cursor movements on desktops,

TABLE 6.1 Features of modeling

Group	Feature
BASE_C (x8)	Repeat, DownRightSpeed_C, Replacement, MaxSERPdepth, DownFreq_C, DownLeftFreq_C, UpFreq_C, UpLeftFreq_C
BASE_A (x7)	Repeat, DownRightSpeed_C, JaccardSimilarity, AveClickDepth, DownSpeed_M, LeftSpeed_M, DownLeftSpeed_C
QUERY (x13)	QueryNum, UniQueryNum, AveCharLength, AveTermLength, correct, generalization, new, parallel, repeat, replacement, specification, QVR, JaccardSimilarity
CLICK (x5)	ClickNum, AvgClickDepth, SatisfiedClick, DissatisfiedClick, MaxSERPdepth
CURSOR&MTI (x20)	Freq_C (x6), Speed_C (x6), Freq_M (x4), Speed_M (x4)
GAZE (x4)	FixationCountPCT, FixationDurationPCT, AvgSaccad

116 Cross-Device Search Behavior Modeling

touch interactions on mobile devices, and gaze movements are implicit indicators of user attention. Features of the CURSOR&MTI and GAZE groups were included in modeling cross-device search behavior under different motivations, since there is a correlation between motivation and attention (Robinson et al., 2012). The CURSOR&MTI group comprises 20 features related to frequency and speed of cursor movement or MTI in various directions. The GAZE group contains four features about fixation and saccade.

6.2.2 Dataset

Although searching both before and after the device transition constitutes a cross-device search, the current modeling concentrates on understanding cross-device searching as an independent behavior, ignoring the intrinsic impact of the device. Hence, we developed the model based on the whole search process rather than the division of pre-switch and post-switch sessions. We modeled cross-device search behavior using data collected from the experiment introduced in Chapter 5, with features calculated based on the whole cross-device search process. The purpose of modeling was to distinguish cross-device search behavior under different motivations. The input was a variety of behavior features, and the output was the motivation. In this case, we acquired 59 samples from the experiment, consisting of 14 samples of P-C, 12 samples of P-M, 17 samples of F-C, and 16 samples of F-M.

Due to the imbalanced sample size of each motivation situation, oversampling is adopted as the resolution of processing data of imbalanced learning (Zheng, Cai, & Li, 2015). The oversampling was conducted by the sampling algorithm embedded in Office Excel. Samples were selected randomly and duplicated to increase the original dataset. Finally, the dataset was comprised of 80 samples, with an equal 20 samples from each motivation situation.

6.2.3 Classifier

We developed the model using the machine learning method, which is popular in areas of both search behavior modeling and motivation prediction. Aiming to model cross-device search behavior under different motivations, we predicted the motivation using the features in Table 6.1 as predictors. Targets involved four motivations of two dimensions: Planned and Forced of controlled motivation, and Memory and Complement of autonomous motivation. We performed binary classification to forecast the motivation of controlled and autonomous dimensions separately.

To select the classifier, we compared the performance of three algorithms: Logistic Regression (LR), Support Vector Machine (SVM), and C5.0 Decision Tree (C5), which work well with small-size learning. The regression method was constantly applied to predict user motivation (Jiang, Rosenzweig, & Gaspard, 2018; Schaekermann et al., 2017). Mitsui, Liu, Belkin, and Shah (2017) treated the problem of identifying intentions as a binary classification problem and used simple logistic regression as the classifier. The SVM has advantages regarding binary classification problems, although it is difficult to explain the behavior with a model trained from the SVM. Decision trees are effective for search behavior modeling, as shown by Tyler and Teevan (2010). The structure of the tree clearly shows what constitutes cross-device search behavior under different motivations. Decision trees and SVM have been used in predicting student's academic motivation (Babić, 2017) and user intent in information-seeking conversations (Qu et al., 2019).

We used baseline features of the BASE_C and BASE_A groups to learn baseline models of controlled and autonomous motivations. Three classifiers were compared by the performance of the baseline models. We ran these machine learning algorithms using IBM SPSS Modeler 18. In order to decrease the influence of a small-sized dataset, five-fold cross-validation was applied when training the models. The original dataset was randomly and equally divided into five subsets. Among these subsets, one subset was used for testing the model, and the remaining four subsets were used as training data. Then, the cross-validation process was repeated five times.

Metrics suitable for multi-label classification problems were adopted to evaluate model performance, including accuracy, precision, recall, and F1 score. Accuracy is defined as the number of correctly predicted labels (TP + TN) divided by the union of predicted and true labels for every utterance (P + N). Precision is defined as the number of correctly predicted labels (TP) divided by predicted labels (TP + FP). Recall is defined as the number of correctly predicted labels (TP) divided by true labels (TP + FN), with F1 as a harmonic mean. These metrics provide an overall performance evaluation for all utterances. Results of the baseline model learned by three algorithms (see Table 6.2) show that C5 outperformed among three classifiers, achieving the highest F1 score in testing. Therefore, C5 was selected to execute the formal modeling of cross-device search behavior.

6.2.4 Training

C5.0 Decision Tree (C5), which outperformed when developing baseline models, was utilized in the formal modeling. Since the modeling was treated as a binary classification problem, we performed the classification for two rounds following the same procedure as the baseline modeling. One round was for modeling cross-device search behavior under controlled motivation (Planned vs. Forced), and the other round was for search behavior under autonomous motivation (Memory vs. Complement). To explore important features that can distinguish cross-device searching under different motivations, multiple models were trained based on different combinations of feature groups, as shown in Table 6.3. The dataset was split into two subsets, training (70%) and testing (30%). Similar to baseline model training, fivefold cross-validation was applied. We obtained 16 models individually for cross-device search behavior under controlled and autonomous motivations, where M1 was the baseline. Comparing the model performance of M2-M16 with the baseline M1, we were able to analyze feature importance.

TABLE 6.2 Baseline model performance of three classifiers

		Training			Testing		
		LR	SVM	C5	LR	SVM	C5
Controlled Motivation (Planned vs Forced)	TP	18	18	17	11	12	14
	FN	7	7	8	4	3	1
	FP	10	9	5	1	1	0
	TN	20	21	25	9	9	10
	Accuracy (%)	69.09	70.91	76.36	80.00	84.00	96.00
	Precision (%)	64.29	66.67	77.27	91.67	92.31	100.00
	Recall (%)	72.00	72.00	68.00	73.33	80.00	93.33
	F1 Score (%)	67.92	69.23	72.34	81.48	85.71	96.55
Autonomous Motivation (Memory vs Complement)	TP	19	20	22	10	10	14
	FP	5	4	2	6	6	2
	FN	6	8	15	1	2	1
	TN	25	23	16	8	7	8
	Accuracy (%)	80.00	78.18	69.09	72.00	68.00	88.00
	Precision (%)	76.00	71.43	59.46	90.91	83.33	93.33
	Recall (%)	79.17	83.33	91.67	62.50	62.50	87.50
	F1 Score (%)	77.55	76.92	72.13	74.07	71.43	90.32

Cross-Device Search Behavior Modeling **119**

TABLE 6.3 Models and corresponding features

Model	Feature
M1	BASE
M2	BASE + QUERY
M3	BASE + CLICK
M4	BASE + CURSOR&MTI
M5	BASE + GAZE
M6	BASE + QUERY + CLICK
M7	BASE + QUERY + CURSOR&MTI
M8	BASE + QUERY + GAZE
M9	BASE + CLICK + CURSOR&MTI
M10	BASE + CLICK + GAZE
M11	BASE + CURSOR&MTI + GAZE
M12	BASE + QUERY + CLICK + CURSOR&MTI
M13	BASE + QUERY + CLICK + GAZE
M14	BASE + QUERY + CURSOR&MTI + GAZE
M15	BASE + CLICK + CURSOR&MTI + GAZE
M16	BASE + QUERY + CLICK + CURSOR&MTI + GAZE

6.3 Analysis of Model Performance Change

6.3.1 Cross-device Search Behavior Model of Controlled Motivation

We trained 16 models of cross-device search behavior under controlled motivation based on different combinations of feature groups. F1 scores of these models are presented in Figure 6.1 for the purpose of model evaluation. M1 was the baseline, and M2-M16 were developed by adding different feature groups to the baseline features. By comparing the F1 scores in testing, there were six models outperforming the baseline: M5, M7, M8, M12, M14, and M16. For adding one feature group, the outperformance of M5 (BASE + GAZE) indicated gaze behavior could help predict controlled motivation of cross-device searching. For adding multiple feature groups, M7, M8, M12, M14, and M16 sharing the QUERY group implies the importance of query characteristics in differentiating cross-device searching under Planned or Forced motivations. Moreover, it can be concluded the more features included, the better model performance achieved.

6.3.2 Cross-device Search Behavior Model of Autonomous Motivation

The F1 scores of 16 models of cross-device search behavior under autonomous motivation are shown in Figure 6.2. In terms of F1 scores of testing, five models were found to outperform the baseline M1, including M7, M12, M13, M14, and M16. For adding one feature group, no model showed better performance than the baseline. It

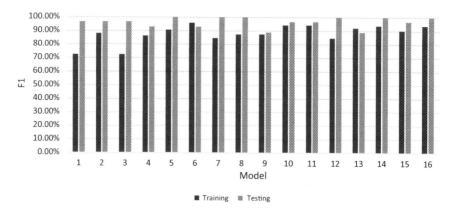

FIGURE 6.1 F1 scores of search behavior models of controlled motivation

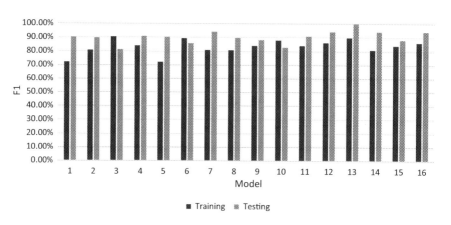

FIGURE 6.2 F1 scores of search behavior model of autonomous motivation

can be inferred that different types of behavior are required to distinguish cross-device search under the Memory and Complement motivations. Query-related features play an important role in modeling cross-device search of autonomous motivation, since five models that outperformed all involved the QUERY group. Furthermore, cursor movements and MTI should also be given importance, because adding the CURSOR&MTI group promoted the performance of M12, M14, and M16. It is noteworthy that M13 achieved the highest F1 score, which indicates the combination of querying, clicking, and gazes contributed the most to optimize the model.

6.4 Analysis of Feature Importance

6.4.1 Important Features of the Superior Model of Controlled Motivation

To analyze important features of cross-device search behavior modeling, we examined the feature importance of the superior model, which indicates the model of best performance. The importance of each feature was calculated as in IBM (2016):

$$\text{importance}_i = \frac{1-p_i}{\sum_i (1-p_i)}$$

where p is the p-value of homogeneity of variance test. The higher the value of importance, the more likely it is that the feature is correlated with cross-device search behavior under a particular motivation.

Comprehensively considering the F1 scores of training and testing, M15 and M16 both achieved the best performance. Further investigation of the structure of these models yielded the same results. Thus, M16 was regarded as the superior model of cross-device search behavior of controlled motivation. The feature importance of M1 and M16 is compared in Figure 6.3. In the structure of M16, baseline features of DownLeftFreq_C and MaxSERPdepth remained, and additional features related to cursor movements, query length, and MTI frequency were included. Features of the CURSOR&MTI group occupied the majority and ranked as having the highest importance, expressing that cursor movements and MTI are of value in understanding cross-device search behavior of controlled motivation.

6.4.2 Important Features of Superior Model of Autonomous Motivation

M13 was considered to be the superior model of cross-device search behavior of autonomous motivation due to its having the highest F1 testing score. Figure 6.4 shows the comparison of feature importance between M13 and the

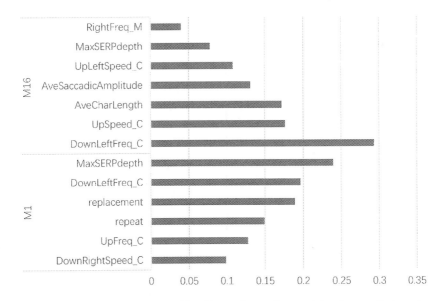

FIGURE 6.3 Feature importance of baseline and superior models of controlled motivation (Note: M1 refers to baseline model and M16 refers to superior model)

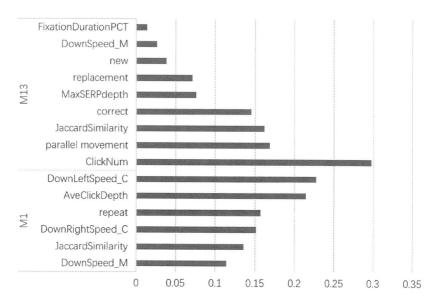

FIGURE 6.4 Feature importance of baseline and superior models of autonomous motivation (Note: M1 refers to baseline model and M13 refers to superior model).

baseline. Clearly, M13 consisted of more features than M1. M13 shared features of JaccardSimilarity and DownSpeed_M with M1 and included more features related to click count, query reformulation, SERP depth, and fixation duration. Specifically, features of query reformulation accounted for the majority of the model structure. This prompted us to attach more importance to users' query reformulation when distinguishing cross-device searching under Memory and Complement motivations.

6.5 Summary

This chapter performs cross-device search behavior modeling under controlled and autonomous motivations using the cross-device search behavior features covered in Chapter 5, with the aim of analyzing the important behavioral features that distinguish cross-device search under different motivations.

This chapter reviews the methods of search behavior modeling, and finds that early behavior modeling is mainly theoretical, using qualitative research methods. With the progress of data collection and analysis technology, quantitative methods (mainly statistical modeling and machine learning modeling) are widely used. The method of machine learning is utilized to train the model in this chapter.

The behavior modeling in this chapter is actually a binary classification problem, and the output involves four types of motivations in two dimensions: Planned and Forced motivations in the controlled motivation dimension; and Memory and Complement motivations in the autonomous motivation dimension. The measures of cross-device search behavior investigated in Chapter 5 are taken as model features, in which the measures that are significantly influenced by controlled motivation or autonomous motivation are grouped into the baseline feature group, while other behavioral measures are grouped into corresponding feature groups. Three machine learning algorithms commonly used in the field of search behavior modeling and motivation prediction, namely Logistic Regression (LR), Support Vector Machine (SVM), and C5.0 Decision Tree (C5), were compared using the baseline features to train the baseline model. The results show that C5 achieves the best performance, so it was selected to train the model with different combinations of feature groups.

By comparing the performance differences between models of different feature combinations and the baseline model, the important feature groups of modeling cross-device search under different motivations are identified. Further, by analyzing the structure of the superior model with the best performance, important features are identified (see Table 6.4).

The results show that, from the perspective of important feature groups, eye movement and query behaviors are of great value to the optimization of a cross-device search behavior model under controlled motivation. Meanwhile, the combination of queries, clicks, and eye movements contributes the most to the optimization of a cross-device search behavior model under autonomous motivation. From the perspective of the important features that are involved in the superior model, cursor movement and MTI are of great significance to distinguish cross-device search under different types of controlled motivations. Also, features of query reformulation play an important role in distinguishing cross-device search under different types of autonomous motivations.

TABLE 6.4 Summary of important feature groups and features of cross-device search behavior models under controlled and autonomous motivations

Motivation	Important Feature Group	Important Feature
Controlled Motivation (planned vs. forced)	CURSOR&MTI	DownLeftFreq_C
		UpSpeed_C
		UpLeftSpeed_C
		RightFreq_M
	QUERY	AveCharLength
	GAZE	AveSaccadicAmplitude
	CLICK	MaxSERPdepth
Autonomous Motivation (memory vs. complement)	QUERY	parallel movement
		JaccardSimilarity
		correct
		replacement
		new
	CLICK	ClickNum
		MaxSERPdepth
	CURSOR&MTI	DownSpeed_M
	GAZE	FixationDurationPCT

Reference

Babić, I. Đ. (2017). Machine learning methods in predicting the student academic motivation. *Croatian Operational Research Review, 8*, 443–461.

Burkhardt, D., Pattan, S., Nazemi, K., & Kuijper, A. (2017). Search intention analysis for task- and user-centered visualization in big data applications, *Procedia Computer Science, 104*, 539–547, doi:10.1016/j.procs.2017.01.170.

Cao, W., Zhang, X., Xu, K., & Wang, Y. (2016). Modeling online health information-seeking behavior in China: The roles of source characteristics, reward assessment, and internet self-efficacy. *Health Communication, 31*(9), 1105–1114. doi:10.1080/10410236.2015.1045236. Epub 2016 Feb 9. PMID: 26861963.

Ellis, D. (1989). A behavioral approach to information retrieval design. *Journal of Documentation, 46*, 318–338.

Foster, A. (2004). A nonlinear model of information-seeking behavior. *Journal of the Association for Information Science and Technology, 55*, 228–237. doi:10.1002/asi.10359

Furner, J. (2004), Conceptual analysis: A method for understanding information as evidence, and evidence as information. *Archival Science, 4*(3–4), 233–265.

Han, S., He, D., & Chi, Y. (2017). Understanding and modeling behavior patterns in cross-device web search. In *Proceedings of the Association for Information Science and Technology* (pp. 150–158.) doi:10.1002/pra2.2017.14505401017

IBM. (2016). IBM SPSS Modeler 18.0 Algorithm Guide. Retrieved from 15th March 2021. https://www-01.ibm.com/support/docview.wss?uid=swg27046871#en

Jiang, Y., Rosenzweig, E.Q., & Gaspard, H. (2018). An expectancy-value-cost approach in predicting adolescent students' academic motivation and achievement. *Contemporary Educational Psychology, 54*, 139–152.

Kim J. Y., Craswell, N., Dumais, S., Radlinski, F., & Liu, F. (2017). Understanding and modeling success in email search. In *Proceedings of the 40th International ACM SIGIR Conference on Research and Development in Information Retrieval* (pp. 265–274). doi:10.1145/3077136.3080837

Kinley, K., Tjondronegoro, D., Partridge, H., & Edwards, S. (2014), Modeling users' web search behavior and their cognitive styles. *Journal of the Association for Information Science and Technology, 65*, 1107–1123. doi:10.1002/asi.23053

Kotov, A., Bennett, P. N., White, R. W., Dumais, S. T., & Teevan, J. (2011). Modeling and analysis of cross-session search tasks. In *Proceedings of the International ACM SIGIR Conference on Research and Development in Information Retrieval* (pp. 5–14). doi:10.1145/2009916.2009922

Kuhlthau, C. C. (1993). *Seeking meaning: A process approach to library and information services.* Norwood, NJ: Ablex.

Lin, S. J., & Belkin, N.J. (2000). Modeling multiple information seeking episodes. In *Proceedings of the 63rd Annual Meeting of the American Society for Information Science* (pp. 133–147).

Lincoln, Y. S., & Guba, E. G. (1985). *Naturalistic inquiry.* Beverly Hills, CA: Sage.

Mitsui, M., Liu, J., Belkin, N. J., & Shah, C. (2017). Predicting information seeking intentions from search behaviors. In *Proceedings of the 40th International ACM SIGIR Conference on Research and Development in Information Retrieval* (pp. 1121–1124). doi:10.1145/3077136.3080737

Montañez, G. D., White, R. W., & Huang, X. (2014, November). Cross-device search. In *ACM International Conference on Conference on Information & Knowledge Management*, China (pp. 1669–1678). doi:10.1145/2661829.2661910

Qu, C., Yang, L., Croft, W. B., Zhang, Y., Trippas, J. R., & Qiu, M. (2019). User intent prediction in information-seeking conversations. In *Proceedings of the 2019 Conference on Human Information Interaction and Retrieval* (pp. 25–33). doi:10.1145/3295750.3298924

Rha, E. Y., Mitsui, M., Belkin, N. J., & Shah, C. (2016). Exploring the relationships between search intentions and query reformulations. In *Proceedings of the Association for Information Science and Technology*, (pp. 1–9). doi:10.1002/pra2.2016.14505301048

Robinson, L. J., Stevens, L. H., Threapleton, C. J. D., Vainiute, J., McAllister-Williams, R. H., & Gallagher, P. (2012). Effects of intrinsic and extrinsic motivation on attention and memory. *Acta Psychologica*, 141(2), 243–249. doi:10.1016/j.actpsy.2012.05.012.

Savolainen, R. (2019). Modeling the interplay of information seeking and information sharing: A conceptual analysis. *Aslib Journal of Information Management*, 71(4), 518–534. doi:10.1108/AJIM-10-2018-0266

Schaekermann, M., Ribeiro, G., Wallner, G., Kriglstein, S., Johnson, D., Drachen, A., Sifa, R., & Nacke, L. E. (2017). Curiously motivated: profiling curiosity with self-reports and behaviour metrics in the game "Destiny". *Proceedings of the Annual Symposium on Computer-Human Interaction in Play* (pp. 143–156). doi:10.1145/3116595.3116603

Spink, A. (1996). Multiple search sessions model of end-user behavior: An exploratory study. *Journal of the Association for Information Science and Technology*, 47, 603–609. doi:10.1002/(SICI)1097-4571(199608)47:8<603::AID-ASI4>3.0.CO;2-X

Spink, A., Griesdorf, H., & Bateman, J. (1999). A study of mediated successive searching during information seeking. *Journal of Information Science*, 25(6), 477–487. doi:10.1177/016555159902500604

Spink, A., Wilson, T., Ellis, D., & Ford, N. (1998). Modeling users' successive searches in digital environments: A national science foundation/British library funded study. *D-Lib Magazine*, 4(4).

Tyler, S. K., & Teevan, J. (2010). Large scale query log analysis of re-finding. In *Proceedings of the 3rd ACM International Conference on Web Search and Data Mining* (pp. 191–200).

Wang, H., Song, Y., Chang, M. W., & Chu W. (2013). Learning to extract cross-session search tasks. In *Proceedings of the 22nd International Conference on World Wide Web* (pp. 1353–1364).

Wang, Y., Huang, X., & White, R. W. (2013, February). Characterizing and supporting cross-device search tasks. In *ACM International Conference on Web Search & Data Mining*, Italy (pp. 707–716). doi:10.1145/2433396.2433484

White, R. W., & Horvitz, E. (2014). From health search to healthcare: explorations of intention and utilization via query logs and user surveys. *Journal of the American Medical Informatics Association*, 21(1), 49–55. doi:10.1136/amiajnl-2012-001473.

Wilson, T. D. (1997). Information behavior: An interdisciplinary approach. *Information Processing and Management*, 33(4), 551–572.

Wu, D, Dong, J, Tang, Y, & Capra, R. (2020). Understanding task preparation and resumption behaviors in cross-device search. *Journal of the Association for Information Science and Technology*, 71, 887–901. doi:10.1002/asi.24307

Yang, C., Yan, H., Yu, D., Li, Y., & Chiu, D. M. (2017). Multi-site user behavior modeling and its application in video recommendation. In *Proceedings of the 40th International ACM SIGIR Conference on Research and Development in Information Retrieval* (pp. 175–184). doi:10.1145/3077136.3080769

Zach, L. (2005). When is "enough" enough? Modeling the information-seeking and stopping behavior of senior arts administrators. *Journal of the Association for Information Science and Technology*, 56, 23–35. doi:10.1002/asi.20092

Zheng, Z., Cai, Y., & Li, Y. (2015). Oversampling method for imbalanced classification. *Computing and Informatics*, 34(5), 1017–1037.

7

DISCUSSION AND CONCLUSION

7.1 Characteristics of Cross-device Search Topics Revealing Information Needs

Information retrieval evaluation campaigns like TREC use the term "topic" to describe a scenario for concrete information seeking, which is represented by task type and topic. Similarly, we regard topic as a broad term that is similar to the concept of task. In Chapter 3, we investigated the attributes of cross-device search topics and analyzed the characteristics of such topics. From the descriptions and surveys of users' cross-device search experiences, we coded 15 categories that can be regarded as attributes constituting cross-device search topics. Specifically, we analyzed these attributes to gain insight into the characteristics from aspects of the topic itself and topic context. Moreover, these characteristics can reflect information needs associated with cross-device searching.

The subjects of cross-device search topics reflect the needs for information content in a cross-device search. The top-searched categories were found to be Arts, Shopping, Reference, and Computers, and we compared these with the findings from previous studies on web searching. Jansen, Liu, Weaver, Campbell, and Gregg (2011) identified the top categories as Society, Arts, Computers, and Business in real-time web searches. Beitzel, Jensen, Chowdhury, Grossman, and Frieder (2004) reported that the three most retrieved subjects are Shopping, Entertainment, and Pornography, based on a large-scale web search log. In both cross-device search and general web search, frequently-searched subjects include Arts, Computers, and Shopping. There is little difference in the categories between cross-device search and general web search. Wang, Huang, and White (2013) explored the topical characteristic of cross-device search tasks and found that Books, Celebrities, and Music are searched for across devices more frequently than other topics. Arts includes literature and music, and, thus, their result is consistent with our findings.

DOI: 10.4324/9780429201677-7

Task types reflect the specificity of needs in cross-device searching. Factual tasks represent the most significant proportion, and most cross-device searching is conducted with a specific question in mind. Most users search across devices in order to deal with a concrete problem and expect either a closed or an open solution. According to the frequent task type, we found that users' information needs during cross-device searches are often transparent and straightforward. This is interesting because the task type for cross-device searching is conceived as an exploratory task by Han, Yue, and He (2015). They designed exploratory search tasks in their cross-device search user experiments, while acknowledging the importance of simple search tasks in cross-device searching. They assumed that a search spanning multiple sessions would represent complex information needs. However, our findings tell a different story. It is certainly true that complex information needs are likely to motivate cross-device searching, but simple information needs are believed to occur more frequently.

Topic complexity reflects the complexity of needs in cross-device searching. According to the revised framework of Bloom's Taxonomy (Krathwohl, 2002), the complexity of the knowledge dimension increases along the sequence of factual knowledge, conceptual knowledge, procedural knowledge, and metacognitive knowledge. Meanwhile, the complexity of the cognitive dimension increases as follows: remember, understand, apply, analyze, evaluate, and create. Analysis of topic complexity in cross-device searching focuses on a low level of complexity in terms of the knowledge dimension, and a medium level of complexity in terms of the cognitive dimension. Specifically, most cross-device search topics had the same complexity of factual knowledge in terms of the knowledge dimension, whereas they varied in the complexity of "understand," "apply," and "analyze" in terms of the cognitive dimension. We conclude that cognition is more important than knowledge in terms of distinguishing the complexity of cross-device search topics. According to Gwizdka and Spence (2006), task complexity can be both objective and subjective. It can be understood that the knowledge dimension measures the complexity of search subjects, and the cognitive dimension measures user cognition. This finding implies that the complexity of cross-device search topics is mainly reflected in subjective aspects such as user cognition. Therefore, the evaluation of the complexity of cross-device search topics should primarily consider measures relating to cognition.

The complexity of the revised framework of Bloom's Taxonomy can be related to the four levels of information need, which Taylor proposes (Taylor, 1968), namely: visceral need (Q1), conscious need (Q2), formalized need (Q3), and compromised need (Q4). Q4 is also known as the command level, and Q1–3 are the questioning levels. The command level denotes the status that the user seeks about a specific item that the user has already assumed will satisfy his/her needs. The command level is considered equivalent to the complexity of factual information in the knowledge dimension of the revised framework of Bloom's Taxonomy, which indicates the basic elements that individuals must know. The questioning levels describe an open-ended, dynamic status of information need.

128 Discussion and Conclusion

They are vague and imprecise, and require feedback from the search system to satisfy the user's needs. The questioning levels involve user cognition, which shows an association with the complexity of the cognitive dimension.

We identified eight reasons why individuals perform cross-device searches, reflecting the motivations for switching devices. Understandably, "unsatisfied information needs" was found to be the main reason. It is natural to continue a search when relevant results have not yet been obtained. The second most frequent reason is "complementing existing search results," which is an interesting finding. This reason indicates a situation in which the user obtains relevant results and continues searching in order to find complementary information. This could mean that the initial information need has been satisfied, but the user chooses to generate a new search that is deeper and more detailed. This is consistent with the findings of Jiang, He, Kelly, and Allen (2017). They discovered that a user's state of mind changes over time during a search.

7.2 Effect of Motivation on Cross-device Search Behaviors

Reasons for cross-device search found in Chapter 3 inspired us to explore the relationship between search motivation and cross-device search behavior. Among existing studies, cross-device search under different motivations has rarely been discussed. In Chapter 5, we designed four motivational scenarios involving controlled and autonomous dimensions of motivation. An experiment of cross-device searching under different motivations was conducted to collect data of various behaviors, including querying, clicking, cursor moving, MTI, gazes, and cognition. We performed a two-way ANOVA analysis to find significant effects of motivation on cross-device search behaviors.

Controlled motivation was found to have significant effects on behaviors related to querying, clicking, and cursor movement. The effect size on measures decreased in the following order: Replacement, DownFreq_C, MaxSERPdepth, DownLeftFreq_C, UpFreq_C, and UpLeftFreq_C. Concretely, compared with Forced motivation users, Planned motivation users took more actions of refining queries, viewing deeper SERPs, and moving cursors. This finding is contrary to the assumption that users that foresee a cross-device search would be unhurried in their searching. The interviews reveal this is because the user knew the device transition was coming, he/she was worried about the inconvenience of mobile searching and consciously performed more search actions on desktop. This indicates that, to those who can foresee a cross-device search, device transition is considered to be an obstacle. Analysis of users' subjective evaluations supports this conclusion, and presents a significant impact of Planned motivation on user perception of the difficulty of a cross-device search. Rha, Shi, and Belkin (2017) found that word substitution (a type of query reformulation) was used when users intended to obtain a whole picture of an item. In light of this, when considering cross-device searching under Planned motivation, it can be understood that when the user expects to have a cross-device search, he/she will intend to find more information. This conclusion is also confirmed by MaxSERPdepth under the Planned motivation, indicating users click deeper SERPs to view more results.

Regarding the effect of autonomous motivation, significant effects were observed on query semantics, click depth, cursor movements, and MTI. To be specific, Memory motivation users issued queries of higher similarity, swiped down more quickly on mobile devices, and more frequently moved cursors down-left rapidly on desktops. Meanwhile, Complement motivation users clicked results of deeper rankings and swiped left faster on mobile devices. Clearly, users purposely utilize more similar queries when the search goal is remembering information found previously. Swiping down indicates a reviewing behavior on SERPs, which is reasonable for searchers who would like to recall. Cursor movement speed implies the user's viewing speed, and the down-left direction indicates viewing a new line. It was not surprising that Memory motivation users quickly view snippets on SERPs, because the users became more familiar with the found information. Analysis of users' subjective evaluation supports this by showing a significant effect of Memory motivation on users' perceived familiarity. The findings about characteristics of cross-device search behavior under the Complement motivation are consistent with our general knowledge. Clicking deeper means the user viewed more results on SERPs to find additional information. It is known that searchers prefer to click top results. In a cross-device search, motivated by the goal of complementing existing information, users prefer to view unvisited pages of deeper results after the device transition. Swiping left on mobile usually occurs following a zoom-in, which indicates a careful examination. Thus, it can be seen the cross-device searcher of the Complement motivation viewed SERPs carefully during mobile searches.

Interaction effects of controlled and autonomous motivations were significant on query reformulation and cursor movement. On the one hand, when the user was given advanced notice of a cross-device search, more repeated queries were submitted to help recall information. When facing an unexpected interruption and forced to engage in a cross-device search, the user would more frequently repeat queries to complement information. On the other hand, those who knew of a cross-device search ahead of time moved the cursor down-right more quickly when searching to recall information. Those who were involved in an unexpected cross-device search moved the cursor down-right more quickly when searching for additional information. It is logical for Planned-Memory motivation users to repeat queries and view SERPs rapidly, since they purposed to search for previously-found information. The same trend of querying and cursor moving was witnessed among Forced-Complement motivation users, which can be explained by user cognition, to some extent. There was a significant drop in perceived clarity among these users, which might lead to a confusing status of the search.

In summary, the current study confirms the effects of motivation on cross-device search behaviors. Although the effects of motivation on web search behavior has been studied, our study is the first exploration of cross-device searching. Kotzyba, Schwerdt, Gossen, Krippl, and Nürnberger (2018) investigated how

130 Discussion and Conclusion

different motivational goals affect users' search behavior while conducting search tasks with different complexity levels. The results suggest that motivational goals have a significant impact on specific aspects of search behavior, while other aspects are unaffected. For instance, it was found that users' executed search strategies were not affected. This was partially consistent with some users in our study, who enacted their initial search strategies during the whole search. Other users claimed the designed motivation scenarios had an impact on their search strategies. A study in the context of internet advertising found that clicking behaviors differ according to consumers' various levels of involvement motivation (Chung & Zhao, 2004). Our study also found a significant effect of motivation on clicks during cross-device searching.

7.3 Effective Method of Modeling Cross-device Search under Different Motivations

To gain a better understanding of cross-device searching, we further explored effective methods of modeling cross-device search behaviors under controlled and autonomous motivations in Chapter 6. The method of machine learning modeling was applied, and observable behaviors collected from the experiment in Chapter 5 were used as features. Features were divided into groups of QUERY, CLICK, CURSOR&MTI, and GAZE. Moreover, behaviors that were found to be significantly affected by motivation were grouped in BASE. We firstly trained models using baseline features in order to select the outperforming classifier among Logistic Regression (LR), Support Vector Machine (SVM), and C5.0 Decision Tree (C5). After that, C5 was applied in the formal modeling with baseline features added with different combinations of feature groups.

We examined the performance improvement of models of controlled motivation. Features related to gaze made an outstanding contribution when adding one type of behavior to the baseline. Other models that gained better performance than the baseline shared features related to query, which indicates query characteristics are important in distinguishing cross-device search under different types of controlled motivation. For models of autonomous motivation, query-related features also play an essential role in improving performance. In addition, model performance was promoted by adding features of cursor movement and MTI. It can be seen that query characteristics should be given importance when modeling cross-device search behavior under both controlled and autonomous motivations. In the field of information retrieval, queries are regarded as a representation of search intention, and their relationships have been widely studied (Mitsui, Liu, Belkin, & Shah, 2017; Rha, Mitsui, Belkin, & Shah, 2016). Search intention and search motivation are correlated, as they both reflect the user's information need. Therefore, it is understandable that query characteristics are important when modeling cross-device search behavior under different motivations.

Considering both the model performance of training and testing, we selected superior models of controlled and autonomous motivation separately and analyzed the feature importance. In terms of controlled motivation, the superior model contains features related to cursor movement, query length, saccadic amplitude, SERP depth, and MTI. Features of the CURSOR&MTI group occupied the majority and ranked the top importance, which implies cursor movements and MTI are valuable in understanding cross-device search behavior of controlled motivation. Regarding the superior model of autonomous motivation, features included characteristics of query similarity, query reformulation, click count, SERP depth, MTI, and fixation duration. Features of query reformulation accounted for the majority of the model structure, which inspires us to attach more importance to user's query reformulation when distinguishing cross-device search under different types of autonomous motivation. The superior models indicate effective methods of modeling cross-device search under different motivations. Cursor movement and MTI should be taken into account when modeling cross-device search under the controlled motivation. Meanwhile, query reformulation is informative when modeling cross-device search under the autonomous motivation.

7.4 Implications of Cross-device Search under Different Motivations

Exploration of cross-device search topics suggests different motivations to search across multiple devices, which generates different characteristics of cross-device search behavior. This can enlighten researchers regarding search task design of cross-device search studies. In a laboratory experiment, participants are likely to be confused about the search goal and information need of a task, which might lead to careless and hasty searches. Our findings suggest that search task design should take motivation into consideration and provide a description of the motivational scenario. Moreover, relationships between motivation and other attributes of cross-device search topics cannot be ignored. For example, correlations found between *Switching Reason* and *Device Switch/Complexity of Cognitive Dimension* indicate that, given a device switch direction or the level of task complexity of the cognition dimension, it is reasonable to provide a corresponding motivational scenario.

The findings of motivation effects on cross-device search behaviors and the effective modeling method can inspire the design and evaluation of interactive information retrieval systems. Cross-device searching under different motivations presents different behavioral characteristics, which can be used to improve the contextual sensitivity of a search system. For instance, searches by Memory and Complement motivation users were different in terms of query semantics, click depth, cursor movement, and MTI. If the system detects queries of high similarity, quick swiping down and rapid down-left cursor movements, the user is likely searching for information to help his/her memory. At this time, the search system can provide means of reminding users about previously issued queries or visited results. By highlighting the role of motivation in affecting cross-device search behaviors, it is necessary to identify more fine-grained search system

132 Discussion and Conclusion

evaluation metrics tailored to different search motivation scenarios. Moreover, certain features were found to be more predictive of motivation than others. This can inform search system implementers about how data-logging capability affects the type of motivations they can capture and analyze.

7.5 Insight on Cross-device Search Studies

Users' cross-device interactions, including cross-device searching, have drawn the attention of Internet service providers from multiple fields, such as search engines, social networks, and e-commerce. In July 2018, Google Analytics launched a new product, called "Cross-device Report," which allows developers to connect data across devices so they can gain a better understanding of users. The open data about Google users' cross-device behavior encourages researchers to study users' cross-device behavior. They can organize user behavior data across multiple devices and perform correlation analysis to learn more about how many seemingly unrelated touchpoints, conversations, and interactions are actually correlated. Likewise, Facebook offers a similar product, called "Cross-device Reporting," which provides companies and businesses with data on the cross-device behavior of Facebook users. Clearly, the search engine and social networking industry places much importance on analyzing cross-device information behavior. The current study explored cross-device search behavior under different motivations, which complies with this trend, revealing characteristics of cross-device search under specific situations. This provides a basis for increasing search systems' contextual sensitivity, allowing them to provide users with accurate information services.

In the field of e-commerce, the study of users' cross-device search behavior is also very important. Criteo, the marketing and advertising consulting company, interviewed 3,300 retailers worldwide, analyzed 1.7 billion online transactions of $720 billion in sales, and found that 58% of transactions involve two or more devices. In everyday life, users commonly search and browse a product on a computer, and then search for and order it on a smartphone. In this case, the user is also a consumer. Understanding cross-device search behavior, including motivations, goals, and behavioral characteristics, can shed light on not only consumer behavior studies, but also marketing and advertising. One of the implications of cross-device searching is that companies and brands should pay attention to the essential role of search visibility in marketing (Miklosik, Evans, & Zak, 2021). Brands and products should not only be visible when consumers initially search for information, but should also remain visible during evolving queries in order to remain considered throughout the whole search process.

7.6 Conclusion

With the increased popularity of smartphones and other devices that can be used for searching, cross-device search behavior is of great interest to information retrieval researchers. This book explores cross-device searching by developing cross-device search topic collection, analyzing the effects of motivation on cross-device search behaviors, and modeling cross-device searches under different motivations.

With respect to cross-device search topics, a crowdsourcing survey was conducted to collect descriptions of real-situation cross-device searches. Based on 343 valid replies to the survey, content analysis was used to identify the attributes of cross-device search topics. The coding scheme was grounded in the MISE model and was revised during coding training. Following two interceding rounds, 15 attributes were coded and analyzed. Attributes reveal the characteristics of cross-device search topics in terms of the topic itself and the topic context. Further, the characteristics of tasks reflect the characteristics of information needs. We have discussed the characteristics of information needs in relation to the need for information content, the specificity of needs, the complexity of needs, and the motivations for switching devices. The subject of information need in cross-device search is somewhat different from that of general web search. In most cases, information needs in cross-device searching relate to a specific question, which means that users are often clear about what they expect to search for. Information needs in cross-device searching present different levels of complexity in terms of the knowledge and cognition dimensions. For the knowledge dimension, information needs focus on the complexity of factual knowledge, which is equivalent to the command level (the compromised need, Q4) in Taylor's four levels of information need. For the cognition dimension, information needs can be of different complexity, such as "understand," "apply," and "analyze." This variety is similar to the questioning levels (Q1–3) in Taylor's four levels of information need, in which the information need level moves between visceral need (Q1), conscious need (Q2), and formalized need (Q3). The most frequent motivation for switching devices is unsatisfied information needs. Statistical tests were conducted to examine the correlation among these. Correlations between attributes can inspire the development of cross-device search topic collection, suggesting that more consideration be given to combining correlated attributes.

With respect to the effects of motivation on cross-device search behaviors, we designed different motivation scenarios based on the findings of attributes of cross-device search topics and conducted a laboratory experiment. On the basis of the self-determination theory (SDT), the adopted motivations were extracted into two dimensions of controlled and autonomous motivation. Fifty-nine university students were recruited to collect behaviors of querying, clicking, cursor movement, MTI, gaze, and cognition during the process of cross-device search. Various measures were applied to analyze these behaviors, and we compared these behaviors under different motivations in terms of the pre-switch search, post-switch search, and the whole search process. A two-way ANOVA was used to test the significant effect of motivation on observable search behaviors. A paired-samples T-test was applied to analyze the significant effects of motivation on subjective evaluation. Results found significant effects of controlled motivation on behaviors related to querying, clicking, and cursor movement. For those who

134 Discussion and Conclusion

can foresee a cross-device search, device transition is considered to be an obstacle due to worry about the inconvenience of mobile searching. Thus, the user consciously performed more search actions on the desktop. On the other hand, significant effects of autonomous motivation were observed on query semantics, click depth, cursor movement, and MTI. Memory motivation users issued queries of higher similarity and viewed snippets on SERPs faster, because they became more familiar with the information found during the search. Interaction effects of controlled and autonomous motivations were found to be significant on query reformulation and cursor movement. We discussed the potential reasons for these significant effects and examined the findings of related studies in a web search context. Our findings partially support some existing studies; for example, the effect of motivation on users' search strategies and clicking behavior.

With respect to modeling cross-device searches under different motivations, a method of machine learning modeling was applied, and observable behaviors collected from the laboratory experiment were used as features. Behaviors that were found to be significantly affected by motivation were regarded as baseline features. We first select the outperforming classifier by training models using baseline features. After that, a C5.0 Decision Tree (C5) was applied in the formal modeling with baseline features added with different combinations of other features. An effective modeling method was found by comparing model performance changes. Considering both the model performance of training and testing, we obtained effective models of controlled and autonomous motivation separately and analyzed the feature importance. Features related to cursor movement and MTI accounted for the majority structure of the controlled motivation model, and query reformulation was found to be informative in modeling cross-device search under autonomous motivation. The findings from the motivation effects on cross-device search behaviors and the effective modeling method provide implications about the design and evaluation of interactive information retrieval systems.

Limitations should be acknowledged. One major limitation is the accuracy of answers to recall-based questions in a crowdsourcing survey of real-situation cross-device searches. Respondents were required to describe their latest cross-device search experience at the beginning of the survey and to answer the subsequent questions according to that latest search. We did not specify a time limitation to define "the latest," because it would restrict the collection of responses. We attempted to make the results of the survey trustworthy by reviewing descriptive texts of the latest cross-device searches. Invalid responses were excluded if the recall had too few details of searching and if the description was short. Despite this, it was difficult to guarantee the degree to which respondents answered accurately. Another limitation is the small scale of participants in the laboratory experiment. Although the total number of 59 participants is within a range consistent with other user studies, the number included for each motivation is relatively small. Natural limitations of laboratory experiments cannot be avoided. Since the effect of motivation on cross-device search behaviors has rarely been studied, we believe the current study, even with some limitations, can help fill this gap.

Future work aims to extend the current study in terms of the theoretical framework and data analysis. SDT is a comprehensive theory consisting of several minor theories. Only a portion of it was adopted in the current study, and more aspects are worthy of excavating, such as the relationship between intrinsic/extrinsic motivation and cross-device searching. In addition to SDT, other classic theories of psychology, social science, education, etc., can be applied in the study of cross-device search in order to expand the boundaries of this area. Furthermore, although mixed-method analyses were used, the qualitative analysis was relatively weak in the current study. In future work, a deeper qualitative study is needed to provide explanations of behavior characteristics found in quantitative analysis, and to develop mental models of cross-device search under different motivations.

7.7 Summary

This chapter first discussed the results of empirical studies. According to the results of cross-device search topics, this chapter discussed the characteristics of cross-device search information needs through the characteristics of cross-device search topics. The subjects of the cross-device search topics reflect the need for information content. Task types reflect the specificity of needs, and the complexity of topics reflects the complexity of needs. According to the analysis of cross-device search behaviors under different motivations, this chapter discussed the effects of controlled and autonomous motivations on cross-device search behaviors and the reasons for the effects. According to the cross-device search behavior modeling, this chapter discussed the effective features of modeling cross-device search under controlled and autonomous motivations.

Implications of the results can enlighten researchers regarding the search task design of cross-device search studies, and inspire the design and evaluation of interactive information retrieval systems. Further, broader insight into cross-device research was discussed in terms of its essential role in Internet information services and marketing. Then, this chapter discussed limitations and future work. Two major limitations of this method are the accuracy of answers to recall-based questions in a crowdsourcing survey and the small scale of participants in the laboratory experiment. The current study should be extended in terms of theoretical framework and qualitative analysis.

References

Beitzel, S. M., Jensen, E. C., Chowdhury, A., Grossman, D., & Frieder, A. (2004, July). Hourly analysis of a very large topically categorized web query log. In *The 27th Annual International ACM SIGIR Conference on Research and Development in Information Retrieval*, UK (pp. 321–328). doi:10.1145/1008992.1009048

Chung, H., & Zhao, X. (2004). Effects of perceived interactivity on web site preference and memory: Role of personal motivation. *Journal of Computer-Mediated Communication*, *10*(1). doi:10.1111/j.1083-6101.2004.tb00232.x

Gwizdka, J., & Spence, I. (2006). What can searching behavior tell us about the difficulty of information tasks? A study of web navigation. *Proceedings of the American Society for Information Science and Technology, 43*(1), 1–22. doi:10.1002/meet.14504301167

Han, S., Yue, Z., & He, D. (2015). Understanding and supporting cross-device web search for exploratory tasks with mobile touch interactions. *ACM Transactions on Information Systems, 33*(4), 1–34. doi:10.1145/2738036

Jansen, B. J., Liu, Z., Weaver, C., Campbell, G., & Gregg, M. (2011). Real time search on the web: Queries, topics, and economic value. *Information Processing and Management, 47*(4), 491–506. doi:10.1016/j.ipm.2011.01.007

Jiang, J., He, D., Kelly D., & Allen, J. (2017, March). Understanding ephemeral state of relevance. In *Conference on Conference Human Information Interaction and Retrieval*, Norway. (pp. 137–146). doi:10.1145/3020165.3020176

Kotzyba, M., Schwerdt, J., Gossen, T., Krippl, M., & Nürnberger, A. (2018). The effect of motivational goals on information search for tasks of varying complexity levels. In *2018 IEEE International Conference on Systems, Man, and Cybernetics (SMC)* (pp. 2602–2607). doi:10.1109/SMC.2018.00445.

Krathwohl, D. R. (2002). A revision of Bloom's taxonomy: An overview. *Theory Into Practice, 41*(4), 212–218. doi:10.1207/s15430421tip4104_2

Mitsui, M., Liu, J., Belkin, N. J., & Shah, C. (2017). Predicting information seeking intentions from search behaviors. In *Proceedings of the 40th International ACM SIGIR Conference on Research and Development in Information Retrieval* (pp. 1121–1124). doi:10.1145/3077136.3080737

Miklosik, A., Evans, N., & Zak, S. (2021). Research on cross-session and cross-device search: A systematic literature review. *IEEE Access, 9*, 82550–82562. doi:10.1109/ACCESS.2021.3086767.

Rha, E. Y., Mitsui, M., Belkin, N. J., & Shah, C. (2016). Exploring the relationships between search intentions and query reformulations. In *Proceedings of the Association for Information Science and Technology* (pp. 1–9). doi:10.1002/pra2.2016.14505301048

Rha, E. Y., Shi, W., & Belkin, N. J. (2017). An exploration of reasons for query reformulations. In *Proceedings of the Association for Information Science and Technology* (pp. 337–346.) doi:10.1002/pra2.2017.14505401037

Taylor, R. S. (1968). Question-negotiation and information seeking in libraries. *College and Research Libraries, 29*, 178–194. doi:10.5860/crl_29_03_178

Wang, Y., Huang, X., & White, R. W. (2013, February). Characterizing and supporting cross-device search tasks. In *ACM International Conference on Web Search & Data Mining*, Italy (pp. 707–716). doi:10.1145/2433396.2433484

INDEX

Note: Page numbers in **bold** refer to tables.

Amanda Spink 12
amotivation 67
Anomalous State of Knowledge 11, 65
autonomous motivation 67
autonomy 66

berry-picking 12

C5.0 Decision Tree 116
classifier 116
click count 87
click depth 89
command level 127, 133
competence 66
Complexity of Cognitive Dimension **31**, 32,
    41–48; analyze 24, 45; apply 24, 45; create
    24, 45; evaluate 24, 45; remember 24, 45;
    understand 24, 45
Complexity of Knowledge Dimension **31**, 32,
    41–48; conceptual knowledge 23; factual
    knowledge 23; metacognitive knowledge
    23–24; procedural knowledge 23
contextual sensitivity 131–132
controlled motivation 67
cross-device 3
cross-device access and fusion engine 56
cross-device computing 14–15, 17
cross-device interaction 14–17, 51,
    63–64, 132
cross-device search 2, 4, 14–17, 61–64
cross-device search patterns 55

cross-device search-related algorithms 56
cross-device search system 51
cross-device taxonomy 14–15
cross-device tracking 53
cross-screen 3
cross-screen tracking 53
cross-session search 3, 61–63, 114
crowdsourcing 24–25
cursor movement frequency 91, **92**
cursor movement speed 91, **92**, 129

Dervin 11–12, 65
device switch 21, **32**, 36
device transition 4
dissatisfied clicks 87–89

expectancy-value theory 68
exploratory search 5, 10–12
exploratory task 33
external regulation 66–67
extrinsic motivation 66–67
eye tracking 96; fixation 98–99; saccade
    98–99

factual task 33
features 115
fivefold cross-validation 117
the frequency of MTI **95**

Hidden Markov Model (HMM) 16, 64, 114
hierarchy of needs theory 10

138 Index

identified regulation 66–67
important feature 120–121
INFEX Framework 15–16
information exploration 10, 11, 64
information foraging 12
information need 10–12, 20, 65, 126–128, 133
Information Search Process 11, 65, 113
integrated regulation 66–67
intention 65
interactive information retrieval system 131, 134
interpretive task 33
intrinsic motivation 66
introjected regulation 66–67

Jaccard similarity 85

Krathwohl 23, **24**, 29, 45, 127
Kuhlthau 11, 65, 113

Logistic Regression 116

Marchionini 5, 10–11
Markov chain 16
Maslow 10
metrics: accuracy 117; F1 score 117; precision 117; recall 117
model performance 119
motivation 36, 64–70
motivational puzzle 65
motivational scenarios: Complement 68; Forced 68; Memory 68; Planned 68
MTI speed **95**–96
multi-screen collaboration 52
multi-session search 61–63
multi-session task 62
Multiple Information Seeking Episodes (MISE) 13–14, 30, 47, 62, 114; episode 12–13, 30, **32**, 39, 62; information problem 12–14, 30, 32, 61–62, 64, 114; information-seeking process 30, **31**, 39; problematic situation 13, 30, **31**, 62

oversampling 116

post-switch session 12
pre-switch session 12

query length 78–81
query number 78–81
query reformulation 81–84
query semantics 85–87
query vocabulary richness (QVR) 85
question negotiation framework 65; compromised need 127; conscious need 127; formalized need 127; visceral need 127
questioning level 127, 133

re-finding 16–17, 62; *see also* re-search; re-retrieval; re-access; revisit
relatedness 66
the revised framework of Bloom's Taxonomy 23, **24**, 29, 45, 127

satisfied clicks 87–89
search behavior modeling 113–114
search genres 14
search session 3, 12
search strategies 103
search task design 131
search visibility 132
segment 4
self-determination theory 66–68
sense-making 10–12, 64–65
SERP depth 87–89
subjective evaluation: clarity 102–103; confidence 102–103; difficulty 102–103; familiarity 102–103
successive search 4, 12–14, 61–62
superior model 120
Support Vector Machine 116

task continuation 63
task interruption 62
Taylor 20, 65, 127, 133
topics 20–48; complexity 23, 34; difficulty 23; subject 21, 32; task type 21–23, 32–33

uncertainty 11, 65

Printed in the United States
by Baker & Taylor Publisher Services